Publisher's Message for
BEYOND INCARCERATION

To shed light on today's cultural, social, economic, and political issues that are shaping our future as Canadians, Dundurn's **Point of View Books** offer readers the informed opinions of knowledgeable individuals.

Whatever the topic, the author of a **Point of View** book is someone we've invited to address a vital topic because their frontline experience, arising from personal immersion in the issue, gives readers an engaging perspective, even though a reader may not ultimately reach all the same conclusions as the author.

Our publishing house is committed to framing the hard choices facing Canadians in a way that will spur democratic debate in our country. For over forty years, Dundurn has been "defining Canada for Canadians." Now our **Point of View Books**, under the direction of general editor J. Patrick Boyer, take us a further step on this journey of national discovery.

Each author of a **Point of View** book has an important message and a definite point of view about an issue close to their heart. Some **Point of View Books** will resemble manifestos for action, others will shed light on a crucial subject from an alternative perspective, and a few will be concise statements of a timely case needing to be clearly made.

But whatever the topic or whoever the author, all these titles will be eye-openers for Canadians, engaging issues that matter to us as citizens.

J. Kirk Howard
President
Dundurn Press

D0874956

A Note from the General Editor
Confronting the Irony of "Correctional Services"

In this exposé, Paula Mallea brings all evidence needed to demonstrate how irreconcilable conflicts exist between publicly stated official goals versus actual institutional performance in our country's so-called correctional services. Drawing on her own experience, Mallea makes a persuasive case for fresh approaches so officials and prisoners alike can break free from the straitjackets of old-fashioned thinking.

Today, this gap between goals and performance remains as glaring as ever. United Nations policy on solitary confinement of a prisoner for more than fifteen days is that it is tantamount to torture, something prohibited by international law. In Canada, prisoners are routinely isolated for much longer periods, even though Canada proudly claims devoted adherence to the United Nations. Within our country, provincial and federal governments still announce improvements in prison operations that never achieve liftoff in the institutions.

When I wrote *A Passion for Justice*, a biography of Canada's greatest law reformer James C. McRuer, an entire chapter was devoted to his work with fellow royal commissioners Agnes Macphail and Joseph Archambault investigating why so many prison riots were taking place across Canada. Long after the commission issued its report and recommendations, McRuer remained haunted, he told me, by the nightmarish scenes he'd witnessed. Yet parliamentarians were unsympathetic. They hounded MP Macphail in the Commons for "misplaced sympathies." In time the seven different types of flesh-tearing whips then used in Canada's prisons were abolished, though other recommendations languished. Those in office saw no voter reward for dealing with offenders — other than getting "tough on crime" and building more prisons.

There's a direct line between these reformist instincts and the impetus here for transforming "correctional" services today. For a country presenting itself as a model for the world, for Canadians coveting a cohesive modern society, for a land where entrenched residential schools imprisoning Indigenous children could be abolished and reconciliation begun, another change is now due. With the force of facts, Paula Mallea's manifesto makes clear it's time to advance beyond incarceration.

J. Patrick Boyer
General Editor
Point of View Books

BEYOND INCARCERATION

Other Point of View Titles

Irresponsible Government
by Brent Rathgeber
Foreword by Andrew Coyne

Time Bomb
by Douglas L. Bland
Foreword by Bonnie Butlin

Two Freedoms
by Hugh Segal
Foreword by Tom Axworthy

Off the Street
By W.A. Bogart
Foreword by Sukanya Pillay

Charlie Foxtrot
by Kim Richard Nossal
Foreword by Ferry de Kerckhove

Sir John's Echo
by John Boyko
Foreword by Lawrence Martin

Dynamic Forest
by Malcolm F. Squires
Foreword by John Kennedy Naysmith

BEYOND INCARCERATION

Safety and True Criminal Justice

PAULA MALLEA

Foreword by Catherine Latimer

DUNDURN
A J. PATRICK BOYER BOOK
TORONTO

Copyright © Paula Mallea, 2017

All rights reserved. No part of this publication may be reproduced, stored in a retrieval system, or transmitted in any form or by any means, electronic, mechanical, photocopying, recording, or otherwise (except for brief passages for purpose of review) without the prior permission of Dundurn Press. Permission to photocopy should be requested from Access Copyright.

Cover image: Shutterstock.com/Tribalium
Printer: Webcom

Library and Archives Canada Cataloguing in Publication

Mallea, Paula, 1949-, author
    Beyond incarceration : safety and true criminal justice / Paula Mallea ; foreword by Catherine Latimer.

(Point of view)
Includes bibliographical references.
Issued in print and electronic formats.
ISBN 978-1-4597-3852-2 (softcover).--ISBN 978-1-4597-3853-9 (PDF).--ISBN 978-1-4597-3854-6 (EPUB)

    1. Imprisonment--Canada. 2. Prisons--Canada. 3. Criminals--Rehabilitation--Canada. 4. Criminal justice, Administration of--Canada.
I. Title. II. Series: Point of view (Dundurn Press)

HV9960.C2M35 2017   365'.971   C2017-904949-6
                                             C2017-904950-X

1 2 3 4 5   21 20 19 18 17

Conseil des Arts du Canada   Canada Council for the Arts   Canada   ONTARIO ARTS COUNCIL / CONSEIL DES ARTS DE L'ONTARIO / an Ontario government agency / un organisme du gouvernement de l'Ontario

We acknowledge the support of the **Canada Council for the Arts**, which last year invested $153 million to bring the arts to Canadians throughout the country, and the **Ontario Arts Council** for our publishing program. We also acknowledge the financial support of the **Government of Ontario**, through the **Ontario Book Publishing Tax Credit** and the **Ontario Media Development Corporation**, and the **Government of Canada**.

Nous remercions le **Conseil des arts du Canada** de son soutien. L'an dernier, le Conseil a investi 153 millions de dollars pour mettre de l'art dans la vie des Canadiennes et des Canadiens de tout le pays.

Care has been taken to trace the ownership of copyright material used in this book. The author and the publisher welcome any information enabling them to rectify any references or credits in subsequent editions.
                                                — J. Kirk Howard, President

The publisher is not responsible for websites or their content unless they are owned by the publisher.

Printed and bound in Canada.

VISIT US AT

dundurn.com | @dundurnpress | dundurnpress | dundurnpress

Dundurn
3 Church Street, Suite 500
Toronto, Ontario, Canada
M5E 1M2

RICHMOND HILL PUBLIC LIBRARY
32972000682098   YR
Beyond incarceration : safety and true c
Dec. 13, 2017

For prisoners and ex-prisoners everywhere

CONTENTS

FOREWORD

Criminal lawyer Paula Mallea brings much-needed attention to the current dysfunction of Canada's correctional system and suggests avenues for immediate and longer-term reform in her insightful and timely book.

While progress toward just, effective, and humane corrections has been gradual, advances have been made toward recognizing that people are sent to prison *as* punishment and not *for* punishment. Correcting criminal behaviour and providing skills that allow former prisoners to be employed and to make a contribution to society upon their return have been seen as contributing to public safety. Canada's *Corrections and Conditional Release Act*, which came into effect twenty-five years ago, enshrined a rights-based approach to the confinement of people in federal prisons and was regarded as a significant milestone and a model for other countries. The closure of the Prison for Women in 2000 and its replacement with five regional facilities that sought to heal and address the underlying conditions affecting women's criminality represented an important step toward realizing a rehabilitative model of imprisonment.

The last fifteen years, however, have seen a reversal of the progress that had been made. A "tough on crime," pro-victim government brought forward a deluge of legislative reforms and budget cuts that had a devastating effect on federal corrections. As Mallea points out, judicial discretion in sentencing, necessary for the precise tailoring of the punishment to fit the crime, which justice demands, was removed by a series of legislative reforms that imposed mandatory minimum penalties of jail time and victim surcharges.

Changes to the *Criminal Code* also created strong disincentives for those battling mental illness to raise their illness as a defence. This compounded the problem of people with mental illness defaulting into the criminal justice system, arising from an antiquated understanding of the criminal defence of mental illness that was established in England in 1843, and which Canada still uses today. Similarly, the inadequate provision of mental health facilities in civil society has often caused the mentally ill to be diverted into prisons where they do not belong, where they cannot be adequately treated, and where their presence results in greater tensions among prisoners.

Other legislative and program reforms have made it more difficult for prisoners to be released on conditional release and parole, even though the evidence shows this form of graduated and supported reintegration into society to be the safest. With more mandatory minimum sentences requiring federal prison time and fewer options for release, the numbers in federal institutions have increased by more than two thousand people, many in need of mental health support, or about four additional penitentiaries' worth of prisoners, in a relatively short period of time. This has led to significant increases in double-bunking — two prisoners in cells designed for single occupancy — a practice that is risky and against the United Nations' *Standard Minimum Rules for the Treatment of Prisoners*, as well as to massive expenditures on infrastructure and expanded prison capacity. At the same time, prisoners are being denied the opportunities and benefits they had previously, because of legislative, policy, and budgetary changes. Prison farms have been closed. Prisoners are required to contribute to their room and board, while the price of phone calls and other amenities has increased. Access to rehabilitative programs has become more difficult, and waiting times have increased such that many prisoners are not able to complete their corrections plans by the time they become eligible for parole. Even essential services, like medical care, have been stretched too thin.

It is not surprising that the Correctional Investigator's reports during this period pointed to a myriad of problems. He called for improvements in the treatment of mentally ill, aged, female, aboriginal, and vulnerable prisoners. He raised concerns about prison crowding, the use of force, and increasing use of administrative segregation. But these criticisms went unheeded during Prime Minister Harper's government. Even objections from the United Nations regarding our use of solitary confinement failed to attract public attention or to result in any changes.

The prospects of making our corrections system more just, effective, and humane looked bleak. The inhumanity and gratuitous punishment beyond that required by the judicial sentence occurred behind prison bars and so was not visible to

Canadians; and if people are unaware of a problem, they are not likely to press for solutions to it. But courageous prisoners, family members, and justice seekers persisted in pointing out the failings. It took tragic and dramatic incidents, such as the deaths in administrative segregation of Ashley Smith and Eddie Snowshoes, and the death of Matthew Hines following use of force by his guards, for the public to take notice. Media coverage and editorials reinforced concerns. The government's unenthusiastic response to the Ashley Smith coroner's report recommendations led to lawsuits challenging whether the laws and practices around administrative segregation respect the Charter rights of prisoners. Canadians are waking up to the problems.

So we are grateful to Paula Mallea, who has knowledge of the serious problems in our corrections system and is willing to speak out and recommend alternatives. There are clearly better ways of achieving a just, effective, and humane criminal justice system than we currently provide. Two clear areas of focus are on providing effective alternatives for those who should not be imprisoned, and on improving the corrections regime for those who are. Countries like Norway, Sweden, and Germany provide excellent models. Canada should learn to treat rather than to punish those suffering from mental illness. More preventive community-based mental health services need to be available. It is cruel, unjust, and ineffective to rely on antiquated perceptions of mental illness and criminal capacity, as it results in far too many mentally ill prisoners. Mandatory minimum sentences will always lead to unfairness for those whose offences and degree of responsibility warrant a penalty less than the mandatory minimum. Those mandatory penalties also preclude consideration of appropriate community-based alternatives to

incarceration. Canada has been successful in significantly reducing its youth correctional population by restricting custody
to the most serious offences and requiring a consideration of
alternatives, including restorative justice approaches. Mallea's
book gives us much to think about and will, hopefully, propel
the correctional reforms so desperately needed in Canada.

*Catherine Latimer is the executive director of the John Howard
Society of Canada. She spent years as a legal policy analyst for the
federal government, both at the Privy Council Office and as director general of youth justice policy at the Department of Justice.*

PREFACE

My first contact with the penitentiary system came through attendance at a church service at Collins Bay. This was one of the few venues where members of the public could actually mingle with the prisoners and share a coffee and conversation. I learned a couple of things that first day. The men in the room were mainly — not all, but mainly — ordinary people. They were the "boy next door," only with a problem. Their problems most likely involved alcohol, drugs, a mental illness, or previous abuse, and these factors always seemed to be at the base of whatever crimes had been committed. In visiting with the prisoners that first day, I talked to a couple of men who belonged to families I knew from my home. They were, literally, the boys next door.

An incident that I experienced later was a reminder that not all prisoners are the "boy next door," but that there is a curious moral code even among these. "George" was devoted to his faith and never missed church. One day he stood up at the back of the room, all six-foot-four of him — even more impressive because as a kitchen worker he was dressed in white — and addressed those assembled.

He said that there were some young "punks" who were only coming to the service so they could drink the wine. George took a dim view of this and threatened to punish the guilty parties. His exact words were, "There will be some butchery here." Then he stalked out of the room, leaving behind a very shaken group of people. Everyone knew George was an enforcer. He had his own version of morality, and he was more than able to back it up.

Later, during my years as a criminal defence lawyer, I met many boys-next-door and quite a few of the dangerous exceptions. However, I was not convinced then and am not convinced now that our criminal justice system, with its emphasis on incarceration, provides the best means of ensuring public safety, proper treatment of lawbreakers, or even satisfaction for victims. In the following pages, I hope to show how the system we have is failing us, and that another way of thinking about criminal justice is overdue. I look at the alternatives that are available to us and recommend the kind of compassion and care that works so well elsewhere in the world. If as Canadians we are trying to promote respect for human rights and the rule of law, it makes no sense to continue with a system that encourages contempt for both.

The more egregious prison conditions that I describe later in this book are shocking by any standard. I do not try to review all of the situations that call for immediate reform. But what occurs in our prisons on a daily basis — the violence, discrimination, and unhealthy and dangerous conditions — should give the average Canadian pause. These are not nineteenth-century prison conditions that I am talking about. And, ironically, they represent Canada's recent escalating response to a declining crime problem.

The result of incarcerating individuals in such conditions can only be negative, with prisoners being released back to society unrehabilitated and with a heightened sense of bitterness and anger. Yet we continue to adhere to a punishment model. It may be that we resort to imprisonment because prisons are all we know, as though they are an immutable if unpleasant fact of life. It is the aim of this book to refute this position and offer alternatives.

I will be suggesting that we consider the fundamental efficacy (or lack thereof) of the prison system itself. In the meantime, I am recommending that we begin an overhaul of the system by improving conditions, incarcerating far fewer individuals, and providing alternative ways of dealing with offenders, especially where offences are non-violent and victimless. These are first steps and should be implemented without delay.

The Liberal government of Justin Trudeau is sending mixed messages about its plans for the criminal justice system. On the one hand, it emphasizes restorative justice and encourages alternatives to prison. Our current minister of justice and attorney general has publicly mused about freeing up the criminal justice system to tackle truly serious crime, and addressing the underlying factors that influence criminal behaviour. This is very progressive thinking. On the other hand, we have the strange spectacle of the federal government continuing to pour more money into prison expansion.

How can we reconcile these disparate points of view? What can we expect by way of reform, much less a complete re-envisioning of the way we treat those who break the law? Consistent messages and action are required if there is to be any positive change at all.

Replacing the prison system with something new will be a daunting project. Changing such an entrenched system is akin to turning a supertanker. It will take a long time, a great deal of care, and an ability to prevail against overwhelming inertia. These will have to be in generous supply if we are to progress beyond incarceration to adopt a more enlightened and effective approach to those who break the law, whether they cause harm or not.

INTRODUCTION

Kingston Penitentiary (KP) was convulsed by a four-day riot in the spring of 1971. The event captured headlines across the country and caught the attention of Kingstonians, who normally went about their daily lives without thinking at all about the institution within their city limits. Yet the prison was hard to ignore. It squatted directly beside the sidewalk of a busy thoroughfare, abutting one of the tonier developments in the city, and commanding a spectacular view of Lake Ontario and Wolfe Island — a view that the prisoners would never see. Its heavy oak gate boasted a massive brass ring. To gain entrance, you had to reach through the iron bars and thump the brass ring against the door — not a high-tech system, but effective. There were gun towers at every corner. A relic from the past, KP was notorious for containing some of the most dangerous men in the country.

During the KP riot, prisoners took six guards hostage, trashed much of the prison, and severely beat a number of fellow prisoners, two of whom died. It was a pivotal moment in the history of incarceration in Canada. What happened then demonstrates why it is urgent that we rethink the way we deal with those who break the law today.

The problems that precipitated the riot in 1971 continue to persist in 2017. Many prisons are old and crumbling. With inadequate facilities, they are not decent places for people to live. There is serious overcrowding, leading to unhygienic and dangerous living conditions. A shortage of professional staff and curtailed rehabilitation programs result in frustration among prisoners since they are unable to complete their release programs and qualify for parole. Far too many people whose crimes could be dealt with by other means are instead imprisoned in high-security institutions. Making matters worse, those in prison are spending too much of their time in their cells with little to do, while extreme polarization between guards and prisoners produces deterioration in the life of the institution. There is a system of grievances, but it is slow and frustrating.

An inquiry determined that these were the conditions that caused the KP riot. We will see that, although things improved somewhat in the ensuing decades, conditions in the Canadian prison system have recently regressed, because of an ideology that advocates being "tough on crime." This approach shows a preference for long prison sentences and harsh conditions of imprisonment. The concerns expressed in the inquiry are still concerns today.

In 1971, the riot ended with no physical harm to the prison staff who were taken hostage. Their personal belongings were even returned to them. The prisoners surrendered, but did so without having achieved any of their demands. However, a good part of the prison was destroyed and two prisoners died.

The response of the prison system was brutal. Hundreds of prisoners were transferred immediately to the new, unfinished, but already much-feared Millhaven Institution, a maximum-security penitentiary. There they were met by a gauntlet of prison staff who beat them as they entered the prison for the first time. One prisoner talked about being kept in segregation (the "Chinese cell") in Millhaven after the KP riot. He said he was chained up for long periods of time with no clothes on. Guards would dump buckets of cold water on him during the night, to keep him from sleeping.

Perhaps this level of brutality was inevitable, given the long and tortuous history of the penitentiary system. The idea of imprisonment began centuries ago, largely as an alternative to earlier, even harsher punishments meted out to those who broke the law. It was determined that locking people up would be better than maiming, torturing, or hanging them. Mere imprisonment must have seemed a progressive development. But over the centuries prisons developed into an inhumane and counterproductive system, one complicated by many contradictory purposes.

By the nineteenth century, prisons were no longer thought of as simply an alternative to brutal corporal punishment. They were instead intended to be redemptive — a place where wrongdoers could be reformed. When Kingston Penitentiary opened in 1837, it was thought that crime was a social disease. The laziness of the poor and their lack of a moral compass were, it was believed, what led to crime. According to this doctrine, separation, obedience, strict religious instruction, and hard labour were necessary to teach people to respect order and authority. Respect for order and authority was pursued with missionary zeal, which led to extreme treatment that was more likely to break the prisoners than to reform them. Absolute silence, lengthy segregation, and repetitive and pointless labour like the treadmill — all of these were supposed to make prisoners reach a penitential state so they could be safely released back into society.

Despite the assertion that these punishments were meant to do good, an investigative report published in 1849 (the Brown Report) claimed that Kingston Penitentiary was rife with inhumane treatment. It referred to the case of an eleven-year-old boy, Peter Charbonneau, who had been committed to prison for seven years. In the space of eight and a half months, he was lashed fifty-seven times for offences like staring, winking, and laughing. Imagine expecting a small boy to refrain from this kind of behaviour, and then punishing him severely in the expectation that he would somehow thus be "reformed."

This could never happen in the twenty-first century, you say. On the contrary, the notorious case of nineteen-year-old Ashley Smith, whose odyssey through the prison system began at age fifteen when she lobbed some crabapples at a mail carrier, is a shame to us all. Ashley could be difficult and uncooperative. She was known to have mental health problems. Treatment would have been an appropriate approach to take with Ashley. Instead, she was incarcerated and placed in solitary confinement on her first day in custody. Ashley repeatedly tried to harm herself, resulting in interventions by staff and dozens of institutional charges. During her eleven and a half months at Nova Institution in Nova Scotia, there were 150 incidents involving Ashley that staff responded to with use of force. Many of the incidents involved Ashley's propensity for self-harm.

Ashley's one-month sentence stretched into nearly four years in custody, served entirely in isolation. The law requires a review of any period of segregation of more than sixty days. However, in truly Machiavellian style, the Correctional Service of Canada (CSC) took to transferring her to different facilities, which allowed them to restart the clock and so avoid the reviews. At no time was a comprehensive mental health assessment done, although the need for one was clear. In 2007, after seventeen transfers to eight different prisons in the space of eleven months, Ashley took her own life. Guards at Grand Valley Institution watched her as she died.

This is how far we have come in over 150 years. The physical and mental torture of the twenty-first century may take a different form from that of the nineteenth, but it results just the same in severe damage to individuals and unnecessary and cruel loss of life. Ashley was not unique in her desperate response to inhumane treatment at the hands of correctional authorities. We will see that suicide and self-harm are all too common in prison.

The *Criminal Code* says that the fundamental purpose of sentencing is to protect society and to contribute to respect for the law and the maintenance of a just, peaceful and safe society by imposing "just sanctions." It takes pains to emphasize that no one should be deprived of liberty if less restrictive sanctions might be appropriate. It says all available sanctions other than imprisonment should be considered if they are reasonable in the circumstances and consistent with the harm done. At the same time, it clearly states that any and all sanctions are intended to be punishment for the harm done. The punishment model is ingrained and paramount.

This raises a number of questions. Why do we continue to rely so heavily upon the prison system, if our objectives are to improve public safety and uphold respect for the law by imposing just sanctions? Why do we over-incarcerate, when the courts have been given clear instructions to use prisons only as a last resort? Why has imprisonment become the default position for dealing with all of the perceived ills of society, whether non-violent drug use or violent abuse or murder — or jaywalking or sleeping on a park bench? How did institutions for the mentally ill give way to prison as a substitute? Why are drug users treated as criminals rather than as candidates for assistance by the public health system? How can we justify treating children the way Ashley Smith was treated? How can we explain why women and minorities, aboriginal people particularly, now represent the fastest-growing segments in Canadian prisons?

I was living in Kingston during the time of the riot and have been asking myself these kinds of questions ever since. Kingston Penitentiary was an appalling place in which to warehouse men in 1971. Ten years after the riot, I entered the institution to see a client. Escorted to the "hole" (the segregation unit), what I saw there convinced me that the average Canadian citizen would not allow a dog to be housed in those conditions. If a prisoner were not mentally ill when he entered that place, he probably would be within a very short time.

I descended a winding iron staircase to a unit well below the ground. The stone walls were seeping moisture. There was no natural light, just the spitting, humming sound of fluorescent tubes. The atmosphere was overheated, suffocating, and claustrophobic. Guards were minimally co-operative and sometimes hostile. "Keep eyes right, counsellor," they enjoyed telling me, so I would not have to see prisoners in the showers. Men were screaming and throwing food and whatever they could get their hands on. Guards repeatedly slammed metal food trays against metal garbage cans. The noise was unbearable, constant, and inescapable. I was placed in an interview room with a clearly unstable prisoner. There was nothing between me and him but a small wooden table and no guard in sight.

I was shaken by this and subsequent visits although I was by then very familiar with the nine penitentiaries in Kingston. These conditions of confinement could in no way serve to improve public safety. I was certain that the public would never approve if they knew how prisoners were compelled to live. It was equally clear that both guards and prisoners suffered immeasurably in this place.

Canadians are almost certainly not aware of the shocking conditions in Canada's prisons, nor do they realize that it is actually possible for prisoners to be released from these conditions directly to the street. With the physical and mental deprivation created by lengthy segregation, it is highly likely that many such ex-prisoners are time bombs, unable to adjust to a changed society and without the resources to cope. Recidivism is a virtual certainty.

There are those who will never be released. Canada's most notorious killer of children, Clifford Olson, died in the hole in KP in 2011. That was the plan — that he never be released into society where he could abuse and murder more children. I doubt if there is any Canadian who thinks that Olson should ever have been back on the street. Perpetual confinement was the only safe solution. But that fact does not justify the treatment he was afforded. The conditions of his incarceration reflect poorly on the prison system and on all Canadians who share a respect for human rights.

There are also prisoners who need to be permanently removed from society. In my time in the penitentiary system, I knew a number of men who were unquestionably dangerous — to the public, to their victims, and to me. One was so violent I was never allowed to get physically near him, whether we were in the prison or in court. Another sat in a tiny interview room at the Don Jail with his knees practically touching mine and described how he broke arms and legs for a living. One psychotic rapist wrote me a disturbing letter from KP just before his release. He was released only twenty minutes from my house, and he knew where I lived. It is clear to me that there are people who need to be kept apart from society for everyone's good. The questions are how do we identify them, and how should we best treat them.

Equally important is the question of what should be done with the many other, non-violent, prisoners who make up the vast majority of those now incarcerated. There is a common belief that all those who are imprisoned are guilty of heinous and violent crimes — that they are monsters incapable of living a useful and non-criminal life on the outside. But this is not the case.

Many or most prisoners are simply people with deep-seated problems, ones that often go all the way back to childhood. They are the quintessential "boy or girl next door," but they are in pain, whether from previous abuse, mental illness, drug dependency, or another cause.

Without downplaying the seriousness of crime, it can be said that most offences spring from circumstances that the rest of us will never have to deal with, and that by far most offenders are not violent. Those who have committed a violent act have usually done so in spontaneous and ill-advised reaction to events and not due to a deliberate plan. And those who have committed planned and deliberate acts of violence are probably part of the class that needs to be separated from society. But those that are non-violent often have committed crimes that have no victim at all. A person may be convicted of failing to appear in court, or failing to report to a probation officer. In fact, up to 25 percent of police-reported offences fall into this harmless category of "administrative charges." Or an individual may have smoked marijuana, or shoplifted, or taken a car for a joyride. Do we really need prisons to deal with these offenders? Looking at such cases, if we were honest would we not say, "That could have been me"?

For several decades efforts were made to improve Canada's prison system. During the late 1980s and 1990s, a new understanding had been reached between correctional authorities and prisoners that allowed for more humane interaction with better results for all. Prisoners felt less threatened and they reoffended at a lower rate. Guards treated them with more respect and made an effort to be helpful, incidentally lowering their own stress levels.

These improvements, though, deteriorated rapidly after 2006 under a new tough-on-crime approach that dictated longer sentences and harsher conditions of confinement. Many knowledgeable observers have commented in recent years that circumstances have once again begun to resemble those that led to the KP riot. There have been many signals that the prison system as a "correctional" institution has been regressing.

Howard Sapers was the federal prison ombudsman (in the Office of the Correctional Investigator or OCI) from 2004 to 2016. His frustration with the tough-on-crime agenda was evident in an interview he gave in 2012. After many years of recommending changes at the CSC, he still found himself dealing with the same old issues. Double-bunking was increasing, as were violence and tension in the institutions. There were more grievances, programs were no longer readily available, prisoners were not able to make parole, and mentally ill prisoners and those with drug dependency were not receiving the treatment they needed. The incarceration rate was rising although the crime rate was falling. He said the recent erosion of long-standing, evidence-based correctional principles and practices had resulted in a breakdown of the relationship between prisoners and guards. The latter had retreated into security bubbles and no longer had much direct interaction with prisoners. One direct result was a riot at Kent Institution in 2010.

Sapers said that as a society we have become too reliant upon prison as the answer for wrongdoing, when it should be a last resort. In this, he was echoing Parliamentary Secretary to the Minister of Justice and Attorney General of Canada Bill Blair (formerly the chief of police in Toronto) and many others who say bluntly that we incarcerate too many people. There needs to be some kind of benefit to incarceration, especially in view of the billions of dollars it costs. If we do not meet the needs of prisoners, then there will be no increase in public safety. Why do we continue on this doomed path?

Recent events confirm that mistreatment of prisoners is an ongoing problem and that our prison system is failing many individuals. Thirty-three-year-old Matthew Hines died in Dorchester Penitentiary in New Brunswick in May 2016. Like Ashley Smith, he had received no treatment for his mental illness. He appeared confused when he refused to return to his cell and the response by guards was violent. He was struck twice with a closed hand, hit in the head with an open hand, and struck twice by a knee. Then he was pepper-sprayed and ten guards took him to the hole. Although he was under control of the staff, he was pepper-sprayed four more times in the face, then taken to the showers for decontamination. In the course of being manhandled and soaked with water, he slipped and fell. His last words were, "Please, please, I'm begging you."

The subsequent investigation by Ivan Zinger, the recently appointed federal prison ombudsman, found that the CSC had lied to the family about what happened, and had even compromised a potential crime scene by cleaning up the blood. Zinger said the CSC response was "catastrophic" and that the way Matthew died could have felt like waterboarding. A post-mortem found he died from lack of oxygen because of the pepper spray. The nurse on staff did nothing to help. No one was held accountable by the CSC at the time, but, to their credit, the CSC has now accepted all of the recommendations made by the ombudsman. Significantly, the case of Matthew Hines is now being investigated by the RCMP.

At the other end of the country, in March 2017, Timothy Nome was about to be transferred from Kent Institution to Stony Mountain. He says senior prison managers told him he was going to receive a "going-away present." He was subsequently set upon by seven guards who beat him severely, saying these were his "goodbye beats." The same thing had happened to him in 2012, after which one guard was fired and another suspended for similar behaviour.

Any system with such a large power imbalance is bound to be vulnerable to abuse. Some supervision of the federal prison system is offered by the OCI, but it has no power to enforce its recommendations. Oversight of provincial systems is also without teeth. And of course very little of what happens in prison ever becomes known to the public. The media take little interest in how prisons operate, and only the worst of the violence and neglect is ever reported.

The inhumane conditions, abuse, and other injustices that prisoners suffer obviously affect the prisoners themselves, but they also have more far-reaching negative consequences. When prisoners serve long sentences, there is a profound effect on their families and communities. Incarceration produces severe dislocation that tears the fabric of society. If a father is incarcerated, the family often loses its breadwinner, plunging them all into poverty. If it is the mother, then children may be taken into care and the family be broken up for good — it is very difficult for a woman to convince authorities to return her children after she serves a prison sentence. Either way, children lose a parent and the community loses one of its members. The disease and ill health caused by prison conditions also follow ex-prisoners into the community.

The devastating impact of incarceration in Canada's penal institutions is especially felt by certain identifiable populations. Vast numbers of minorities, especially aboriginal people, and women of all backgrounds — out of all proportion to their percentage of the general population — are being incarcerated. In the past decade, the number of aboriginal men and women in prison has shot up by more than 40 percent and 70 percent, respectively. Although they represent only 4.3 percent of the total population of Canada, aboriginal people comprise 25 percent (men) and 35 percent (women) of federal prisoners. Ninety-one percent of the women who are incarcerated have histories of abuse, and many have disabling mental health problems. At the same time, the number of black prisoners in the federal system has increased by 75 percent over a decade. We stand convicted as a people of racism and sexism, so starkly represented by our prison populations.

Also overrepresented in Canada's prisons are those suffering from mental health issues and those needing treatment for drug dependency. And long prison sentences are producing an aging prison population. Our prisons are expected to provide psychiatric, palliative, and long-term care as well as treatment for drug dependency. However, prison staff are not trained or equipped to do these jobs. Individuals with such special needs should be treated outside prison walls, where their support systems are available to them and they are not facing the violence and deprivation of prison life.

Studies have shown that the kinds of social programs that will prevent crime and discourage recidivism can be better delivered outside prison. Victims' rights advocates understand this and recommend community-based programs as a way of preventing more victimization. Vengeance for them is not a high priority, if it is a priority at all. Safety is.

Other countries have rates of incarceration that are much lower than Canada's. They maintain these low levels by respecting the human rights and dignity of those who break the law and by sending only the most serious offenders to prison. Our own Canadian values are surely not reflected in the fact that we have one of the highest rates of incarceration of any Western nation.

We need to take a pause, back up, and look at the bigger picture. How did prison come to be our default mechanism for dealing not just with violence and victimization, but also with things we simply dislike or find annoying? Why are our prisons crammed with people who have committed non-violent, victimless offences? Why are we building more prisons and incarcerating more people when the crime rate has been falling for over twenty-five years?

These are questions that need to be put to policy-makers, but the impetus has to come from the grassroots. In order for that to happen, the public needs to understand what exactly is going on in our prisons and what needs to change. This starts with understanding our system of sentencing.

1

GETTING TO PRISON: SENTENCING

The value and efficacy of the prison system, if any, can be partly tested by the ways in which we sentence people who break the law. The arbitrariness, inconsistency, and inflexibility of sentencing give the lie to any claim that the system in place is fair and just to everyone in conflict with the law, wherever found and no matter their background. Fairness and justice are not always what this system provides.

In an effort to establish more consistency, Canadian legislators set out principles of sentencing in 1996. The law said that sentences were meant to achieve three objectives: to reduce the use of prison as a sanction, to expand the use of restorative justice and other alternatives to prison, and to show sensitivity to the particular circumstances of aboriginal Canadians.

As mentioned earlier, the *Criminal Code of Canada* states that the fundamental purpose of sentencing is to protect society and to contribute to "respect for the law and the maintenance of a just, peaceful, and safe society by imposing just sanctions."

It then sets out a number of objectives that those sanctions are meant to achieve. In order to assess the efficacy of the prison system, it is important to examine whether the sought-after objectives are being met and whether they might be met just as readily without resorting to imprisonment.

The *Code* also says "an offender should not be deprived of liberty, if less restrictive sanctions may be appropriate in the circumstances," and "all available sanctions, other than imprisonment, that are reasonable in the circumstances and consistent with the harm done to victims or to the community should be considered for all offenders, with particular attention to the circumstances of Aboriginal offenders." Despite these clear instructions, it will be seen that judges vary widely in their perception of what is "appropriate" and "reasonable."

Let's compare a couple of cases that involve theft. My client Shannon (I am using pseudonyms throughout), a nineteen-year-old aboriginal woman with a new infant, walked into a department store and took twenty-dollars' worth of baby clothing. She passed the cashier without paying and was charged by the store's security. She appeared in court as required and pleaded guilty to shoplifting. I submitted to the court that she had no criminal record, had a good background as a student, and was raising her child on her own. She was in need of the items she had taken and had no money to pay for them. The store had recovered all of the goods. To the astonishment of everyone in the court room, the judge imposed a jail sentence.

More recently, over two hundred Canadian lawyers were disciplined by their law societies for misappropriating $160 million belonging to victims of abuse at residential schools. Some of these lawyers took funds belonging to the estates of deceased persons, some stole trust funds, and some overcharged the government for their services. Only about twenty of these people have been charged with criminal offences. Everyone else was allowed simply to pay the money back. This was not an option for Shannon.

Similarly, wealthy Canadians who have used offshore accounts to evade paying taxes have been offered an amnesty program by the government. They are allowed to confess and pay back the taxes owing. They are assured they will not be sentenced to prison. This also was not an option for Shannon.

It is clear that white-collar crime is treated differently from the crimes committed by people who are marginalized and poor. We seem to throw the heavy and expensive machinery of the criminal justice system at minor cases and insignificant players, but not at those that involve millions of dollars and often affect the most vulnerable among us. If we can deal with some of these cases without resorting to incarceration, why not the others?

OBJECTIVES OF SENTENCING: ARE THEY ACHIEVED BY INCARCERATION?

The *Criminal Code* sets out six objectives of sentencing. The first is denunciation, which is straightforward and takes effect from the moment a charge is laid. The idea is to convey publicly to both the accused and the victim that society does not approve of the impugned behaviour. Clearly denunciation — public condemnation — could be accomplished with something less than incarceration. We should be thinking about how best to achieve this.

Deterrence is the second objective of sentencing and it is relied upon by Crown attorneys everywhere to argue for increased sentences. Yet we know from evidence that deterrence does not actually work. One meta-analysis done for the solicitor general of Canada in 1999 involved over three hundred thousand prisoners. It concluded that increasing sentence length actually increases the likelihood of recidivism. The study found that there was no empirical support for the proposition that imprisonment deters criminal behaviour. It found that alternative treatment programs were more effective in reducing offending.

Those findings referred to what is called specific deterrence, which applies to the convicted person himself (most are men). The sentence imposed upon him is supposed to be sufficient to deter reoffending. There is also general deterrence. This is designed to discourage others from breaking the law. It presupposes that a potential lawbreaker knows what sentence will likely be imposed for a particular crime and thus will think twice before committing that crime. It also supposes that individuals who break the law are seriously thinking about the possible consequences of their actions. This is demonstrably not the case. Acting impulsively is the hallmark of the average offender. And even those who are part of a deliberate and organized endeavour are not calculating how many years they will serve if caught. They are doing their utmost not to get caught, so the issue never comes up. Recall the old story about young pickpockets working the crowds that gathered in London to watch the hanging of other young pickpockets. On the other hand, if the prospective lawbreaker perceives that there is a likelihood of getting caught, and that the consequences will be more or less immediate, there is some evidence that this may deter the behaviour.

Deterrence also earns a big "fail" when we look at the conditions that often give rise to criminal behaviour. My most excruciating example of our failure as a society and the resulting criminal behaviour is the case of Harrison. Harrison was brought up in a Prairie court on mischief charges. This individual had exhausted his welfare benefits, had no family or friends, and suffered from a mental illness. When he was arrested, he was living in an abandoned car in twenty-below-zero weather. He had tossed a rock through a window because he believed, correctly, that if he went to jail he would be warm and fed. I don't know what became of Harrison, but the prognosis was not good. What does it say about our society that he or anyone would be driven to such extremes just to survive? The whole idea of deterrence is made to stand on its head in these conditions.

Danny was from a family that had been engaged in criminal activity for generations and lived in an area of the city known for its criminal elements. The community was so steeped in a criminal lifestyle that people still used the jargon of crooks from decades ago. They talked of "sawbucks" ($10 bills) and "fins" ($5 bills). Interviewing them was like taking part in a Jimmy Cagney movie.

Danny's life chances were very poor. When I met him, he had been arrested for several break-and-enters. As police officers often do, they charged him with over twenty break-and-enters that had occurred around the same time in the same area. Danny had no idea which ones he had committed, but he was willing to plead guilty to some he remembered if I could arrange for a non-custodial sentence. A reasonable Crown attorney agreed to make the joint submission for no prison term and we went to youth court. As usual, I had told Danny that there were no guarantees because it's not possible to predict what a judge will do, but, I said, the arrangement with the Crown was unusually generous.

The judge in her wisdom disagreed with counsel and sentenced Danny to eighteen months in youth detention. As we left the courtroom, he was barely able to keep back his tears — tears of anger and frustration and betrayal. All he said was, "That's it. No more Mr. Nice Guy." He was thirteen years old. It is safe to assume that Danny went on to grow up in prisons of one kind or another. He had learned that he could trust nobody, including his defence counsel. I expect the sentence imposed by the judge achieved the exact opposite of the deterrence that was intended.

Billie was eighteen and already becoming a "rounder" — someone who had been in and out of prison for years. One day he came to me with a subpoena. He was being asked to give evidence against an acquaintance. What should he do? As his lawyer, I was obliged to advise Billie to respond to the subpoena. However, in his world and among his friends, this would make him a "rat." The consequences could be severe. For certain, he would be despised by everyone who knew him. At the worst, he could be killed. In Billie's mind, he understandably had no choice. The threat of prison time was no deterrent at all.

Billie went to prison for six months for contempt. It was his first time in a real prison (rather than a youth facility). When I next saw him, the quiet, frightened boy I knew was standing tall and confident. He told me that refusing to give evidence and accepting the prison sentence had given him immense stature in his criminal community. For the first time in his life, he had respect. Far from offering a deterrent effect, the prison sentence merely confirmed Billie in his criminality.

Might there be other ways of deterring individuals and the public from committing crimes rather than sending them to prison? Would alternative processes be more successful both for the individual and for his family and community? The answer resides in providing choices to Danny and Billie that are not available to them now, and is a resounding "Yes."

The third objective of sentencing is "to separate offenders from society, where necessary." This is what we call incapacitation, and it is simply meant to ensure that a specific person cannot continue to commit crimes because he is behind bars. This separation objective would appear at first sight to be a slam dunk — of course removing a lawbreaker from society serves the purpose of preventing further crime. But does it really?

There are a number of reasons why removing people from society does not succeed in reducing crime. First of all, we have no way of knowing which people would continue to commit offences if they were sentenced to something other than prison. Many, perhaps most, would not. Thus, it might be just as efficient and effective to allow them to serve their sentence in their community.

As well, putting people behind bars often just opens the way for other aspiring criminals to step up and replace them, perpetuating and often escalating the criminal behaviour. This is known to be the immediate result of imprisoning drug dealers, for example. Countless low-level dealers are anxious to move up in the hierarchy and gain the power that goes with being a kingpin.

In Mexico, this has been well illustrated by the behaviour of the drug cartels. The government there has captured and imprisoned any number of drug lords, only to watch rival cartels battle for the lucrative turf and seek to fill those top positions. Murder, torture, and mayhem have resulted. Well over a hundred thousand people have been killed and tens of thousands are missing. Mass graves are being uncovered on a regular basis. Thus, the capture of single individuals may remove them from society, but it also spawns a shocking level of additional violence.

Offending by an individual does not necessarily stop just because a person is in prison, either. Often, serious offences continue to be committed by the convicted person within the prison: crimes such as murder, extortion, or assault. There is a danger that such offences will be discounted by the public because they occur in prison and their victims are usually other prisoners. It is important to remember, though, they do represent continued offending and their victims are human beings. Our recognition of this is essential to reducing the "us-versus-them" attitude that encourages more rather than less incarceration.

Finally, incarceration cannot be said to succeed in its intention to incapacitate if the result is that a prisoner continues to commit crimes or even escalates his criminal activity upon release. Long prison sentences frequently harden prisoners to the point where they are bitter, antisocial, and ready to wreak their own version of vengeance on a society that has treated them like scum. Recall my description of the hole at Kingston Penitentiary. Think about the many recent reports of the conditions of segregation in prisons across the country. These are the most dehumanizing circumstances that we could possibly invent. They are contrary to international human rights treaties and contrary to our own belief in our values as Canadians. People who are being released after this type of treatment cannot be expected instantly or completely to step back into society, reintegrate with their communities, somehow find employment, and stay out of trouble.

This embittering of prisoners might be less true if the next stated objective of incarceration, the rehabilitation of prisoners, was actually pursued with greater resources. But if that were to happen, the ability of prisons to provide useful rehabilitation is still often overstated. Rehabilitative programs can be provided, and sometimes are, but the atmosphere in prison does not help prisoners to absorb necessary information and lessons, much less to open up in counselling sessions like anger management, or to divulge a history of sexual abuse.

Having said that, there was a time in Canada when the CSC provided extensive and much-admired programs of rehabilitation, many of which had a positive effect on prisoners. It was able to provide these programs for about 2 percent of the CSC's annual budget of $3 billion.

For example, prisoners could take educational programs that alleviated illiteracy and provided some hope of employment upon release. Prisoners could also take university courses, and could even be released to attend classes at university.

I knew one. Brian was convicted of the brutal murder of a young woman at a time when capital punishment was the penalty. A few days before his execution date, his sentence was commuted. Brian served eighteen years in the toughest prisons in the country. At his last location, he was allowed to leave the prison to attend the local university. He was eventually released and lived the rest of his life on parole.

Brian became a respected criminologist with a Ph.D., who contributed to his community in many ways. His rehabilitation was a remarkable example of what can be achieved when the prison system works with prisoners to provide them with the skills they need to live a full and crime-free life on the outside. This is to the advantage of society and public safety as well as to the benefit of the individual. But Brian was an exceptional individual, and he was able to take full advantage of his opportunity. He also had unwavering support from family on the outside. Most prisoners are not so capable or so well supported. They may lack the background, motivation, or ability to take up such a challenge. They may also suffer from a mental illness or a drug problem that prevents them from benefiting from rehabilitation programs.

Today, prisoners are no longer allowed to leave the prison for educational purposes. They are required to pay for any courses they might want to take, with the exception of courses from Grades 1 to 12 and GED preparation courses. Paying for courses is an impossibility for most prisoners. As well, during the 1990s, education programs were reduced because they were thought of as less important to rehabilitation than programs like drug treatment and anger management. Yet the CSC's own follow-up research on the Adult Basic Education (ABE) program showed that for higher-risk prisoners, recidivism dropped by 5 percent to 30 percent if they had taken the ABE equivalency program: a not insignificant result for public safety.

One rehabilitation program acknowledged to be among the most valuable in teaching life skills and work skills was the prison farm. Declaring that farming was not relevant to employability in today's world, the Conservative government closed the farms in the face of vocal public opposition. But the real value of the farms, aside from financial (they provided milk, eggs and other produce for many other institutions), was in the skills and life lessons learned by participating prisoners. Supporters said that the skills learned there were easily transferable to other jobs. Working on the farms promoted a strong work ethic and sense of responsibility, as prisoners learned to take care of cattle and other animals. Tending to the animals also helped the prisoners to have empathy for them. Working with local farmers, the prisoners received something they had often never experienced: respect. Among the many skills they learned were heavy machine operation, time management, self-reliance, safety around machines and animals, responsibility for the animals, and so on.

The CSC had once lauded its farms program. In a 2006 article, it glowingly described the Frontenac Institution farm as a place that made positive changes in prisoners' lives. Despite this analysis, there was a quick about-face with the advent of a Conservative government that same year. The new government was anxious to make life harder for prisoners no matter the consequences and the prison farms were closed in 2010.

Today, the new Liberal government appears to have accepted the rehabilitative value of the farms and is committed to reopening them. A new advisory panel has been established to guide the CSC in reopening the two prison farms in Kingston. It will work with CORCAN, the Correctional Services employment and skills training division. Ironically, one of the members of the new panel, Jeff Peters, himself a farmer, had been incarcerated because of his activities defending the prison farms. He is already suggesting a number of new areas for the prison farms to pursue, from making artisanal cheese to producing solar panels and biogas devices.

Another rehabilitative program lauded by the CSC was Lifeline. This was an award-winning program that provided support for long-term prisoners, helping them serve their sentence with fewer incidents and helping reintegrate them when they were released on parole. Lifers comprise about 20 percent of the prison population, and Lifeline was the only program directed specifically at them. The program operated for twenty years on a budget of about $2 million per year and was admired and emulated by other jurisdictions. The CSC's own evaluation of the program was very positive, showing that prisoners on the program were less trouble both within the prison and upon release, with less recidivism. Nonetheless, the CSC closed Lifeline down in 2012 to save money. The agency defended its actions at the time saying, in direct contradiction of its own research, that the program did not improve public safety.

CORCAN is, according to the CSC website, a key rehabilitation program in the penitentiaries. Prisoners get on-the-job skills training building furniture, learning welding, providing print services, and so on. Most of the products are sold to government departments. The highest pay scale is only $6.90 per day. There has been no wage increase in twenty-five years, while the cost of a basket of goods from the canteen has risen from $8.49 to over $60 during the same period. Perhaps it goes without saying that prisoners are not covered by labour laws. More recently, the incentive pay that prisoners used to receive to support their families on the outside and to facilitate visits and telephone calls has been removed. And, under the Conservative government, prisoners were paying 22 percent of their wages for room and board and 8 percent for the prisoner telephone system. Thus, any real incentive to work for CORCAN and achieve the skills it affords was severely eroded. Also, as of 2015, CORCAN was reducing its number of prisoner employees.

Rehabilitation as an objective of sentencing can be achieved only on a limited basis, and for only some prisoners. Judges, however, often sentence people to a longer term or to a federal penitentiary just because the programs there might be better, or because a longer sentence will give the person more time to take advantage of the programs. As defence lawyers, we have all seen judges take this position while failing to see the harm in extending a prison sentence so arbitrarily.

This strange state of affairs exists primarily because we fail to provide necessary programs to people in their communities before they ever commit an offence. Proper education, work experience, incentives, and strong connections to community and family produce a much better result before the fact than after.

Much has already been written about the need for preventive programming and for governments to recognize the direct line that can be drawn between the provision of adequate social supports and a reduction in the crime rate. It is not the purpose of this book to review the various programs. It is clear, though, that funding should be provided at the front end, before a crime has been committed, where programs have the best chance of success. There would be fewer victims and less harm to everyone involved.

The final purposes of sentencing as set out in the *Criminal Code* are to provide reparations for harm done, and to promote a sense of responsibility in those who break the law and acknowledgement of the harm they have caused. These purposes would be better achieved by a system of restorative justice that is separate from our traditional court system. Reparations can better be provided if the offender is out of prison and working and able to make a contribution. Similarly, a sense of responsibility will come more readily if the offender is confronted face to face with the harm he has done, other than in a courtroom, and is in a position to express himself to the victim and the community — something that is impossible from behind bars.

The tough-on-crime agenda relies largely upon the perceived needs and wishes of victims to justify long and harsh prison sentences. But we will find that in general victims are highly sophisticated in their understanding of the criminal justice system and what it can offer them by way of solace. Most have come to realize that sheer vengeance should have no place in determining consequences for the lawbreaker. Their own ability to handle the harm done to them depends on a different approach.

WHAT DO VICTIMS WANT?

Victims have fought long and hard to be respected and included in the system that adjudicates the people who harmed them. It is easy to make assumptions about what victims want and how to provide it for them. Often it is assumed that vengeance in the form of long and harsh sentences is their main objective. But it would be wrong to pigeonhole them in this way.

Victims generally take a nuanced and balanced approach to the question of sentencing and the appropriateness of imprisonment. They continually surprise us by going beyond their own harm and assessing what might be done to prevent a similar harm to others. There is little evidence that victims generally want harsher sentencing, and studies show the opposite. Even victims of violent crime are no more inclined to be punitive than anyone else.

Heidi Illingworth has been the executive director of the Canadian Resource Centre for Victims of Crime for many years. She has advocated for victims in every important forum in the country and has a deep understanding of what victims need and what works to prevent further victimization. She says it is not the sentence an offender receives that is important to victims. Steven Sullivan, former federal victims ombudsman, also says that the sentence does not make much difference to the situation of a victim. The victim's harm is unlikely to be alleviated by a prison sentence, however harsh. Both agree that what matters is how the justice system treats victims.

Lorraine Berzins knows something about victimhood. She worked in federal penitentiaries for fourteen years and was taken hostage while working in a federal prison. Until 2011, she headed up the Church Council on Justice and Corrections. She argued against longer and harsher sentencing on the basis that this would do even more harm and would not prevent victimization. She said that more incarceration of marginalized people was counterproductive and undermined human dignity in society. It is significant that she refers to the human dignity of society and not just of prisoners — the two are inextricably linked.

Berzins argued at a Senate committee that funding should be directed at the preventive programs that have been shown to work in preventing further victimization: probation, bail options, reporting centres, practical assistance, supportive housing, and all programs that promote accountability, respect, and reparation. She told the government what victims actually want: that wrongdoers take responsibility, realize the harm done, realize that it was wrong, try to do something to repair it, show remorse, and try to compensate in some way. Victims, she said, are concerned about prevention and they want to get on with their lives in the assurance that they will be safe. Our adversarial system of criminal justice militates against achieving these goals.

Arlène Gaudreault, as president of the Association québécoise Plaidoyer-Victimes, argued at the Senate committee against harsher sentences for young people. She said longer sentences do not automatically translate into greater protection for society or for victims. Harsh sentencing is a placebo, and the government should instead attack the risk factors for crime, such as poverty and inequality. In this way, she said the government would be taking the long view, presenting a vision that would actually reduce offending. Gaudreault resented that political parties all seem to exploit victims for their own partisan purposes, mainly to legitimize more crime control. She was adamant that this was not the position of all victims.

Moms Stop the Harm (MSTH) is a network of Canadian mothers and families whose loved ones have died due to substance use. The network calls for an end to the failed war on drugs. The members envision a new approach based upon reducing harm, where people who use drugs are treated with respect, compassion, and support. Their members exhort governments to allow those with drug dependency to obtain the drugs they need. Yes, this would mean giving people heroin and opioids and other drugs in a controlled setting. It would also save lives by preventing dangerously contaminated drugs or overly pure drugs from being consumed, and by largely eliminating the role of organized crime in the drug industry.

These are some examples of how victims recognize the importance of looking beyond the immediacy of conviction and sentence. They particularly understand that if programs were created that prevent offending in the first place, or assist with rehabilitation after the fact, the number of victims would be significantly reduced. This could also be accomplished at much less cost than mass incarceration.

MASS INCARCERATION: THE CAUSES

Mass incarceration has been the direct result of two policies: long sentences, including mandatory minimum sentences (MMSs); and measures that make it harder for prisoners to gain release. The United States has recognized that its current astronomical incarceration rate is largely due to MMSs introduced for numerous offences in past decades, such as victimless, non-violent offences like drug use and possession. During the Obama administration, steps were being taken to redress this situation in the United States. At the same time, however, the Harper government in Canada was introducing even more MMSs.

The new Liberal government under Prime Minister Trudeau has promised to tackle the problem of MMSs, but has been slow to act. Some experts predict that the government will go beyond simply rescinding the MMSs imposed by the previous government and will adopt more fundamental changes to the current sentencing regime. Others are more skeptical. Recent activity on this front has been attributed to a Supreme Court ruling that set down strict limits on the length of time an accused person can wait for his trial. Serious charges were being stayed as a result. The minister of justice said, "Was it a kick in the butt? I think it was a call to action for all of us, absolutely." She then agreed to reduce the number of MMSs in order to get rid of the court backlog, while insisting that MMSs are perfectly appropriate for more serious offences.

Canada's most well-known MMS was adopted as an alternative to capital punishment in the 1970s. In place of the death penalty, Parliament determined that murderers should spend twenty-five years in prison before they could apply for parole. This harsh sentence was later alleviated when Parliament passed the "faint hope" law. This enabled some lifers to apply for parole at fifteen years. It was a successful program. The process was rigorous, and very few of those who were released ever reoffended. Nonetheless, under the recent Conservative government, the "faint hope" law was repealed — it had been adjudged as soft on crime.

Today, a number of MMSs dictate long sentences for drug and firearm offences, among others. But problems arise when minimum sentences are enacted. First of all, a stated purpose of MMSs is that they provide a deterrent to people who might be planning to break the law. But studies have repeatedly shown that MMSs and long sentences, as was noted earlier, generally have no deterrent effect on prospective criminals, and no effect on crime rates. Minimum sentences are the perfect tool for tough-on-crime politicians, but they provide a lazy, cynical, and simplistic approach to policy-making on criminal justice.

MMSs are a bad idea because they completely remove discretion from judges, who are then compelled to impose minimum prison sentences, despite differing circumstances of the individual and the offence. This has prompted some judges to suggest that computers might as well do the job of sentencing.

Grave injustices are often the result of minimum sentences. Years ago, stealing a car would net an offender a minimum of one year, so that even a youthful joyride led inevitably to a sentence of one year. Similarly, there used to be a minimum of seven years for importing drugs. This was so out of touch with reality that Crown attorneys prosecuting in Brampton (the court that covered offences occurring at Pearson International Airport) regularly dropped drug-smuggling charges down to possession-for-the-purpose charges in exchange for a guilty plea and a lesser sentence.

One of my clients was caught at the airport coming back from a Jamaican holiday wearing a body pack full of hashish. In no time at all, she had agreed to a guilty plea to possession for the purpose of trafficking for a three-year sentence, rather than take her chances with a trial and a seven-year minimum. The Prison for Women was full of women serving seven years in the 1970s. The Supreme Court of Canada eventually over-turned this particular MMS as unconstitutional, saying that it would "inevitably result, in some cases, in a legislatively or-dained grossly disproportionate sentence." It also said that it was inappropriate to have to rely upon Crown counsel to find ways around the law.

This is just one way that MMSs are circumvented by the system when it recognizes the potential for injustice. Police of-ficers also sometimes turn a blind eye. Victims refuse to report offences. Juries refuse to convict. Thus, MMSs fail to provide the certainty and consistency that is supposedly intended. Instead, MMSs displace sentencing discretion to another level of the system. This effectively puts police officers and prosecutors in the position of judges — a job for which they are not trained and that they would prefer not to take on.

Mandatory minimums lead to other injustices. Accused persons sometimes plead guilty to a lesser offence, whether or not they are guilty of anything. This is because the thought of being convicted of the full offence, with the lengthy sentence attached, is too much to bear. On the other hand, for those who are not offered a plea to a lesser charge, there is no benefit in pleading guilty. They might as well take their chances with a trial. In such cases, a full trial with motions and technical arguments and appeals will be the result, at great cost to the system, with no appreciably useful result.

Finally, a desperate accused might be pressured to bargain for a lesser charge and sentence in return for giving information that would help police charge a bigger player (such as a drug dealer who is higher up in the organization). This places accused persons between a rock and a hard place — they either have to go for the mandatory minimum or make a deal, assuming the position of a "snitch," and seriously endangering their own prospects for a future.

Recently enacted MMS drug laws have a clear potential for producing manifestly unfair results. For example, if you cultivate 200 marijuana plants, you will receive a sentence of six months minimum, but if you miscount by one and grow 201 plants, you will go to prison for a year. If you do so on rental property, these sentences become nine and eighteen months, minimum.

By way of contrast, justice is much more likely to be achieved when judges are allowed discretion in sentencing. For example, a client of mine was charged with trying to smuggle LSD into Millhaven. The consequences of attempting to bring any drugs at all into the visitor area of such facilities are very serious. Fortunately for my client, however, she was in front of an experienced judge who also knew the ins and outs of the prison system.

The judge was persuaded by the circumstances of this woman's case not to send her to prison for the long period normally imposed. My client was married to one of the prisoners in the institution and they had two small children. Her husband was being pressured by other prisoners to make his wife bring drugs into the prison. If she failed to do so, the consequences for him would be serious and possibly fatal. Both my client and her husband were desperate. He was afraid for his life. She was equally afraid that he might not survive his sentence, leaving her and the children alone. Faced with that situation, she had decided to deliver drugs to the prison. However, now that she had been arrested, there was the likelihood that she would go to prison, too, and that their children would therefore be put into foster care.

The judge, however, ordered her to serve four days in jail. He knew that she would be admitted to the local lock-up and be released almost immediately. She had a friend who could look after the children. This was a case where a judge competently assessed both the accused's circumstances and the seriousness of the situation in which she found herself. Had there been a mandatory minimum sentence, his hands would have been tied.

Robert Latimer was not so lucky. His story illustrates the problems that arise when there is an inflexible rule of sentencing. Mr. Latimer, a Saskatchewan farmer, admitted to killing his twelve-year-old daughter by carbon monoxide poisoning. The girl was a quadriplegic who functioned at the level of a three-month-old. She weighed only forty pounds. She was in constant, excruciating pain that could be treated only with regular Tylenol, and was facing more surgery to correct a hip dislocation aggravated by advanced scoliosis. Mr. Latimer was told that the operation would place her in even greater pain than the intense pain she was already experiencing. After he was charged, Mr. Latimer told police that he loved his daughter and could not bear to watch her suffering. But because what he had done was planned and deliberate, he was charged with first-degree murder.

The trial was a *cause célèbre* for the disabled community, who argued that such behaviour represented open season on the disabled. Two separate juries found Mr. Latimer guilty of second-degree murder, with the second jury recommending he be eligible for parole after one year. The jury clearly assumed the judge had discretion to make such an order. However, this was not the case. There was a mandatory minimum sentence that required Latimer to serve ten years before eligibility for parole.

The sitting judge tried his best to accommodate the jury's recommendation. He drew a distinction between murder and mercy killing and provided Mr. Latimer with a "constitutional exemption," ordering a sentence of less than two years, with one year to be spent in the community. This sentence was appealed all the way to the Supreme Court of Canada, which overturned the decision and reinstated the ten-year minimum eligibility period.

Seventeen years after the offence, Mr. Latimer was finally granted full parole. It took longer than it should have because he believed that he had done the right thing and refused to express the remorse required by the parole board. No remorse:

no parole. Thus, although the trial judge found that he was no threat to society and required no rehabilitation, Robert Latimer paid a heavy price for acting in a way that fell afoul of the law but that many felt was purely compassionate.

There is one last thing that mandatory minimums do which puts judges in an untenable position. The *Criminal Code* requires them not to send someone to prison if less restrictive sanctions are available and appropriate. But how are they to square this fundamental principle of sentencing with the requirements of minimum sentences of imprisonment? This conundrum has never been adequately addressed by our politicians. It is a fatal flaw in the legislation and requires immediate attention.

Allan Manson, an expert in sentencing law, has recommended that a sentencing commission be established that would introduce a measure of coherence to sentencing practices. Others have suggested that the Law Reform Commission of Canada, disbanded early in the Conservative government's mandate, be reinstated and asked to overhaul the *Criminal Code of Canada* — a job that has not been tackled since 1955. This would enable legislators to eliminate the clear contradictions that currently exist in sentencing laws and to place less emphasis on custodial sentences and more on alternatives.

NON-VIOLENT, VICTIMLESS OFFENCES

Before leaving the subject of sentencing, let's look at some of the aberrations, contradictions, and inconsistencies that occur. For a start, judges commonly impose fines that alternatively attract a prison sentence if the individual fails to pay. Thus, the offender might be told to pay a fine of $500 within a set time. If he does not, he will, instead, have to serve a short prison sentence.

But if a judge feels a $500 fine is sufficient to fulfil the sentencing principles of denunciation and deterrence, why is it that the individual can later be deprived of his freedom simply because he is unable to pay the fine? Here is where a fundamental principle of our *Criminal Code* is broken. Either the offence is worthy of a deprivation of freedom, or it is not. If it is not, then the fact that an indigent offender may be unable to pay a fine should not result in his imprisonment. Nonetheless, people go to jail every day largely because of their economic circumstances.

Courts are beginning to find ways of dealing with an apparent class bias that also nets jail terms for what can only be described as annoying behaviour. Recently, a homeless man in Toronto was before the court facing an accumulated balance of $65,000 in fines for offences like jaywalking and loitering. He was manifestly unable to pay. He had stopped drinking and was trying to get his life back on track. The judge understood that jailing him for failure to pay the fines would undo all the positive steps he had taken. With the consent of the Crown, the judge wiped out the fines and put the man on two years' probation instead. This is a model to follow.

There are many other offences that do not merit custodial sentences — especially those that do not involve violence and that create no victims. As mentioned earlier, about 25 percent of charges laid by police are "administrative offences." These are offences against the administration of justice, such as failing to appear in court when required, breaching probation, failing to comply with bail conditions, and so on. The number of charges related to these kinds of offences has risen sharply over the past decade. Where an offender is convicted of a substantive offence (theft, for example), and where there are attached administrative offences, the offender is sentenced to custody 53 percent of the time. For those who have no administrative offences attached, 22 percent go to prison. Courts clearly consider that administrative offences, which supposedly represent a lack of respect for the judicial system, are often more deserving of a prison sentence than the substantive offences to which they are related. Does this make sense?

My client Aaron agreed to bail conditions that included having to report once a week to the local RCMP detachment. He breached this condition but it turned out that he had a good reason. He owned exactly one set of clothes: a jean jacket, a pair of jeans, sneakers, a couple of T-shirts, and a baseball cap. It was February on the Prairies. He owned no coat or parka and no boots. He had no driver's licence, no car, and nobody who could drive him. The police station was three miles from his home. Even so, he had managed the trip for the first few weeks.

Why, you wonder, did he agree to such a condition? Well, because all he knew was that he wanted to be released to go home, and so he was prepared to agree to anything. I should have picked up on this, but it never occurred to me that the circumstances were all wrong for him to be able to make this trip once a week. The breach was inevitable. This time the explanation convinced the judge to change his bail conditions and make them more reasonable, but it was touch and go whether he was going to be incarcerated for showing disrespect to the system.

It is clear that Aaron and others in his position should not have to go to prison for transgression of the conditions set on them and, fortunately for Aaron, in this instance things worked out. There are other areas of criminal law, too, where prison is manifestly inappropriate. What about the many convicted of drug offences that are non-violent and victimless? Why is the solution to lock up the drug user, separating him or her from family and community, and often plunging dependants into poverty, certainly jeopardizing the future of them all? Surely there is a solution outside the prison system that would address use or abuse — essentially a public health issue — without causing such irreparable harm to a wide circle of people.

Even serious property offences could be dealt with by means other than incarceration. My clients Fred and Donna were serious drug users who resorted to petty crime and prostitution to fund their habits. On one occasion, high on cocaine, they went to a jewellery store in downtown Toronto in broad daylight, threw a brick through the window, scooped up some gold jewellery, and made off. They were predictably apprehended within a city block due to the fact that their getaway car got stuck in rush hour traffic and they didn't think of fleeing on foot. This Abbott and Costello routine put them in court on a very serious charge of robbery, conviction for which would entail years in custody, given their previous records.

All of the jewellery in this case was recovered by the owner of the shop, so the only cost to him was the replacement of the broken window. When the matter came up for trial, the shop-owner did not respond to his subpoena. It being a busy Toronto court, the matter was dropped and Fred and Donna were free. Clearly, the shop-owner made a judgement call that it was not worth closing down his business for at least a day to attend in court when he was only out a couple of hundred dollars.

Readers might object at this point that justice was not done here, that the smash-and-grab was a serious criminal offence and that the perpetrators and their behaviour deserved to be denounced. But you have to wonder in whose name the system would be imposing a prison sentence. If the victim was not interested in exacting his pound of flesh, why should we object? At the same time, a complete lack of consequences did not seem to be the right result either. Our rigid system of justice was simply not adequate to the task. There was no way to direct Donna and Fred to community services that might have helped with drug treatment and provided them with an alternative to their current lifestyle. No alternative solutions were available.

Years later, after any number of additional custodial sentences for both of them, I ran into Fred when he was serving a penitentiary sentence and asked him about Donna. He told me that she had been hooking to support her cocaine habit while he was in prison. She went with a john to a high-rise condo. While the john was out of the room, Donna climbed over the railing on the twentieth-floor balcony and jumped.

Donna was a vibrant, beautiful, smart young woman with a serious problem. At no point was her problem ever addressed. The criminal justice system ate her up and spit her out. Other countries and jurisdictions have better ways of dealing with these cases and we need to learn what works and get over our resistance to change.

The process of sentencing is inexact, arbitrary, and manifestly unjust. Yet it daily delivers the most serious consequences imaginable for thousands of Canadians. How do we explain why prison sentences are imposed in one province but not another for identical offences? Why are rural Canadians treated differently from urban Canadians when it comes to explaining the amount of illicit drugs they possess? How can we be appointing judges who are capable of deciding a murder case based upon a section of the *Criminal Code* that has been unconstitutional for years?

We are, in the twenty-first century, very good at punishing those who break our laws. In doing so, we think we are working on behalf of victims, but we have seen that this is a chimera and that victims by and large do not seek vengeance. We also know that punishment for its own sake can breed more criminality. Further, it is imposed on dubious moral grounds, since it is rarely applied to the upper socio-economic classes. Nonetheless, Canadians appear to be convinced that incarceration is an appropriate sanction for all kinds of behaviour. That being the case, it is important that Canadians should know the conditions to which they are consigning thousands of their fellow citizens.

2

PRISON CONDITIONS: DEVELOPMENTS SINCE 1971

It is important to look at conditions in Canadian prisons because many of our fellow citizens have to live there for long periods of time before they are released to live among us. We have to consider what imprisonment does to human beings as a measure of how they will respond to living in society when their incarceration is over. We also have to consider that the world will judge us for the way we treat prisoners.

By and large, those who are incarcerated are among the most marginalized and disadvantaged in society. If we treat them as "other," as people who are somehow lesser, we diminish ourselves as well as them and we will fall into the trap of limiting their human rights. This erodes our approach to human rights across the board. As one prison guard said, if we take away the rights of prisoners, we end up taking away our own rights as well.

Conditions in the federal prison system are controlled by the Correctional Service of Canada. Comparable conditions exist in the provincial systems and are under the aegis of the provincial governments. Canada adopted the *Charter of Rights and Freedoms* in 1982, which guaranteed among other things that there should be no cruel and unusual punishment in the criminal justice system. This was followed in 1992 by the *Corrections and Conditional Release Act*, which was designed to entrench human rights as central to corrections and to ensure the paramountcy of the *Charter*. Further, the Supreme Court of Canada has on numerous occasions emphasized that the rule of law must be paramount within prison walls and that human rights must be placed front and centre.

These developments occurred in tandem with a number of reports on the prison system that were highly critical of its operations and made scores of recommendations for change. The 1971 Kingston Penitentiary riot was the first of many violent episodes (including riots at the B.C. and Laval penitentiaries) that ultimately led to the MacGuigan Report. This report, authored by MP Mark MacGuigan, was pivotal in setting the stage for major reforms in the Canadian prison system. In 1975–1976, there had been sixty-five major incidents in the federal penitentiary system in Canada. In 1977, during the time that MacGuigan committee members were visiting prisons across the country — when prisoners could see that action was being taken on their grievances — there were no incidents at all.

What those committee members saw made a serious impression on them. They concluded that the federal prison system was a failure in two ways — it neither corrected law-breakers nor offered protection to society. There was a shocking 80 percent recidivism rate at the time — today it is less than half that. The report said that imprisonment in Canada was inhumane, destructive, psychologically crippling, and socially alienating. It said vengeance has no place in the system, and that prisoners should be provided with humane treatment and living conditions. It emphasized that when a lawbreaker is sentenced to prison, deprivation of freedom is the punishment. Any additional measures that make prison conditions harsher and tougher are illegal and effectively impose a second prison sentence. This is not part of the CSC's mandate.

The report said that guards are themselves prisoners of a brutalizing system. But it went further, calling some staff at Millhaven hoodlums and describing their behaviour as reprehensible. There was deliberate harassment and brutalization of prisoners, with threats and assaults not unusual. Citing security considerations, staff attempted to justify all kinds of dehumanizing behaviour. Clean laundry might not be available to prisoners for weeks at a time. Counts and recounts might be conducted endlessly, prisoners might be awakened every hour on the hour for no reason, meals might be delayed, or contaminated, or both. In one case, security problems were cited as justification for feeding prisoners only twice a day. MacGuigan said this was deliberate and arbitrary punishment.

I recall seeing a client housed in Millhaven Institution during this time. There had been an incident that had resulted in a lockdown. I had met this prisoner once before and recalled him as a quiet, fit, articulate young man. He was not a troublemaker in the institution. He, like most other prisoners, prided himself on his appearance, hygiene, and courtesy to his lawyer.

When I saw him a few weeks later, during the lockdown, he came into the interview room looking like a shadow of himself. He immediately apologized for the fact that he had not been allowed to take a shower for more than a week. But, worst of all, the administration had taken away his false teeth. We all know what that does to the appearance of an individual. His face was sunken. He looked like an old man and he was unable to articulate properly.

I could not imagine why the administration would do such a thing, other than to humiliate the prisoner. It could not have been done for reasons of security. It was a completely arbitrary punishment, gratuitous and mean-minded. My client was ashamed to be seen by me that day.

MacGuigan said that the experience of imprisonment was itself criminogenic — that is, it actually produces the kind of behaviour that it is trying to control. Those who end up in penitentiaries have already been damaged by a multitude of other agencies — schools, foster homes, group homes, orphanages, the juvenile justice system, the courts, police stations, provincial jails. Most of those in prison were not dangerous, he said, but the various cruelties and humiliations inflicted on them while incarcerated frequently made non-violent prisoners violent, and the dangerous even more dangerous. Incarceration failed in its two purposes: correcting the prisoner and protecting society. In fact, imprisonment itself epitomized injustice.

MacGuigan made a long list of recommendations, including adopting alternatives to incarceration, such as restorative justice. The report said that within prisons the rule of law must prevail in every instance, attention must be paid to the mentally ill and to minorities, human rights must be respected, and work, education, and training should be provided to prisoners.

MacGuigan's report began the long process to a more responsive and responsible prison system. Michael Jackson, a criminologist at the University of British Columbia and expert on the Canadian prison system, recounts the difference between prison operations in the 1970s and later, in the 1990s, when his book *Justice Behind the Walls* was published. The CSC adopted a mission statement in 1989 that set out what might be described as a "moral compass" governing the way staff were to interact with prisoners. There was to be more "normal interaction" and less adversarial behaviour. Some staff responded positively and some did not. Yet there appeared to be an improvement in attitudes and behaviour on both sides.

These improvements were far from universal in the federal prison system, though, and a 1994 incident at the Prison for Women (P4W) in Kingston brought to light again the importance of respect for human rights and the rule of law.

It started when a disturbance at the P4W resulted in strip searches of women prisoners by male emergency responders. They also conducted invasive body-cavity searches (trivialized by guards, who called these "skin fans"). Prisoners were housed in segregation for lengthy periods in appalling conditions. One staff person who worked at both P4W and KP at this time said he was asked by a KP guard, "And how are the cunts over at P4W?" This level of contempt for prisoners seemed to be common among some guards.

Madame Justice Louise Arbour, former Supreme Court Justice and later United Nations Commissioner for Human Rights, was charged with investigating these events. Like MacGuigan's, her 1996 report was excoriating. She started by saying that a prison sentence does not give authorities the right to disregard the very values that criminal law is meant to uphold — honesty, respect for the physical safety of others, and respect for privacy and human dignity. The minimum standards of incarceration set down by the United Nations include clean and decent cells, good food, regular laundry services, exercise, medical care, education, training, work, spiritual support, access to books, radio, and television, counselling, and an ongoing connection with friends and family. Arbour described P4W as inadequate in every way. The prison resembled a maximum-security institution, and deserved its reputation as "unfit for bears."

Arbour severely criticized the attitude of the CSC. She said there was a disturbing lack of commitment to the ideals of justice, including a failure to observe human rights, and that this was embedded within the culture of the CSC. When the emergency response team left the women in their cells, they left them in appalling conditions that had nothing to do with security concerns. They were placed in small, empty cells on a cement floor and were barely covered with a paper gown. There was nothing to sit or sleep on — no blanket, mattress, or towel. Yet the windows were left open (this was in April). They were left in body belts, shackles, and leg irons.

The Arbour Report asserted that the ultimate product of our criminal justice system — imprisonment — itself epitomized injustice. In the face of the CSC's recalcitrance, she recommended a legislated remedy. She said that a prisoner's sentence should be shortened in cases where there had been illegality, gross mismanagement, or unfairness by the CSC. This recommendation has never been acted upon. Her further recommendation that a time limit be imposed upon the use of segregation has also not been adopted.

In 2007, a government document entitled *A Roadmap to Strengthening Public Safety* became the blueprint for the new

Conservative government on all matters correctional. *Roadmap* was produced in an impossibly short six months by people who had no special expertise and it made virtually no reference to the many reports and analyses that had so far been published. There was no acknowledgement of the centrality of human rights or of the paramountcy of the rule of law. *Roadmap* was in fact simply the product of an ideology that believed in being tough on crime.

An exquisite dissection of *Roadmap* was provided by Michael Jackson and Graham Stewart (former executive director of the John Howard Society). Entitled *A Flawed Compass: A Human Rights Analysis of the Roadmap*, their document was a brilliant analysis of the importance of human rights and the rule of law to the prison system. It particularly noted changes in the system between the time of the MacGuigan Report and the 1990s, when the management of prisons had begun to improve. They were able to illustrate these changes by reporting the experiences of people who worked in the system over those years.

One prison guard said when he first went to work at the B.C. penitentiary in the 1970s that the prisons were "so damn dangerous that you were glad to be home any given day." Twenty years later, he knew he would make it home in one piece. He said in the old days it was not safe for officers to walk among the prisoners. Excesses in force were common and there was an almost complete code of silence between staff and prisoners. By the 1990s, they had learned to do things in a better way and it was paying dividends. While some people argued that prisoners had too many rights, this officer said that taking away prisoners' rights meant staff possibly lost the same rights themselves. In other words, respect for human rights for everybody was essential.

Another staff member recalled his first days on the job in 1981. He said guards stood around the courtyard talking about which prisoners they would get rid of — how they could get under their skin. They discussed which one they would shoot and kill if there was ever a riot. In 1995, the officer said, the conversations among staff were completely different. They talked about which programs would help the prisoners, which would best suit certain individuals, how they would deal with an attitude problem and get a prisoner motivated. The approach of staff had changed to the point that prisoners were civil to staff, saying "please," and being polite. Back in the old days, a prisoner would have been more likely to shout, "Hey, you fucking pig."

One long-time officer admitted he no longer thought that having TVs and private visits produced a "Club Fed." He said there were still consequences for misbehaviour, but there were not so many hostage-takings and riots as in earlier days. He added that if we want to protect society, we do not want to release prisoners to the street after years of harsh treatment.

This is wisdom from people who have spent years in the system and have seen and practised two diametrically opposite approaches. They have clearly decided that the more progressive and humane, less violent and vengeful approach will provide better public safety.

Other changes over those decades made a big difference to the atmosphere in prisons and to the declining number of violent incidents. For the first time, women were now being hired on staff. This tended to improve communication and the quality of interaction between staff and prisoners. Also, in the twenty years or so after the KP riot, the "con" and "bull" codes were broken. These were the codes that dictated minimal communication between prisoners (cons) and guards (bulls), rude and profane responses where possible, complete contempt and lack of respect for one another, and no interaction that presaged an actual human relationship, much less friendship or mentorship. These codes guaranteed an almost completely dysfunctional system and justified any amount of violence and mayhem as prisoners and guards attempted to exert their own versions of control. Once these codes were broken, staff benefited from improved training and were now motivated to work with prisoners in a positive way, reducing the confrontational atmosphere. As one long-time prisoner said, "Most of the staff got rehabilitation on their mind instead of slamming you up and telling you to shut the fuck up."

Despite these improvements, however, the CSC largely continued business as usual. Its overuse of segregation, despite multiple recommendations to stop this practice, is one example of how difficult it was to get the CSC to change. Many managers focused on "fixing the optics" when a problem arose rather than trying to find solutions. And today, after those brief few years when there was some real improvement in interactions between staff and prisoners, the prisons are run pretty much as they were fifty years ago.

In fact, in many ways the prison system has been deteriorating. Responding to *A Roadmap to Strengthening Public Safety*, the CSC adopted a "Transformation Agenda" that provided for much harsher conditions of imprisonment and much less likelihood of prisoners achieving release on parole. Immediately, the climate within the prisons shifted in a disturbing way, according to critics Jackson and Stewart. Prison staff were given the green light by the Conservative government to toughen up conditions. Prisoners describe hardened attitudes and confrontational behaviour. They began to have less access to the yard or the gym. They were routinely strip-searched after visits. Maximum-security institutions now practise lengthy confinement to the cells, making them resemble super-max Special Handling Units (SHUs). One long-time prisoner, bank robber Stephen Reid, described the more recent atmosphere as "callous."

Among the most reliable sources of information about federal prison conditions are reports produced by the nonpartisan Office of the Correctional Investigator (OCI). This prison ombudsman is charged with providing oversight of the CSC by investigating complaints in the federal prison system. Howard Sapers was the ombudsman from 2004 to 2016, and his office has been scrupulous in investigating complaints about the federal prison system and recommending solutions.

His most recent annual reports express a growing sense of frustration and even despair about the trends he observes within the system. Only a couple of years after implementation of the "Transformation Agenda" by the CSC, Sapers's 2009–2010 report noted that the prison population was increasing. Prisoners were spending more time in custody and harsher prison conditions were being imposed. They were confined to their cells for longer periods of time, all movements were more highly controlled, and there was less access to the prison yard, recreation, and crafts. Correctional officers ("COs" or "guards") had less interaction with prisoners, retreating behind barriers and control booths, and there was an alarming increase in "use of force" incidents where guards used force against prisoners — a 25 percent increase in one year.

Most prisoners were no longer being released on parole, but were exiting the system much later, at two-thirds of their sentence, as required by law, on "statutory release" or SR. Prisoners are released on SR because they are regarded as too much of a risk to be released on parole. This is usually because they have been unable to complete their core correctional programs — a prerequisite for consideration for parole. There are now huge backlogs for such rehabilitation programs, and some programs like the prison farms have been shut down. (As noted earlier, plans are under way to reopen at least some of these.) For women, an important Mother-Child program was restricted so that the numbers of women participating declined by 60 percent.

The ombudsman cited double-bunking as a reason for rising tensions and violence in the institutions. Self-injury incidents were rising, and suicides were a continuing scourge. Segregation was being overused for all segments of the population, including those with mental illness. A growing number of prisoners were now elderly, and the institutions were not providing appropriate services for them. The increase in numbers of women and aboriginal prisoners was alarming, and programs to help deal with their special needs were not keeping up. Likewise, mental illness and drug dependency both required special attention, but there were not enough resources to provide good services to the populations affected.

The following year, Sapers noted that the number of complaints received from prisoners by his office had increased by 36 percent over two years. Conditions of incarceration were hardening. Only 1.8 percent of the CSC budget was devoted to programs. Yet Sapers noted that every dollar spent on programming returned $4 in saved incarceration costs.

Meanwhile, research suggested that when proper programming was available there could be up to a 60 percent reduction in recidivism, thus enhancing public safety.

By 2012, the level of OCI's frustration with the CSC was rising as the Conservative government passed new laws that ordered the CSC to use "necessary and proportionate" measures in dealing with prisoners, replacing the "least restrictive" principle. This opened the door to the CSC imposing punishments and reducing privileges and incentives. But, as Sapers pointed out, the CSC is not authorized by law to add further punishment to the sentence. It is supposed to administer the sentence imposed by the court and to prepare prisoners for the future. It is mandated to provide rehabilitation programming to prisoners.

By 2013, the ombudsman was making direct comparisons with the conditions that led to the 1971 Kingston Penitentiary riot. He wrote that many of the same problems leading to the riot over forty years before continued to be a part of contemporary correctional practice. Sapers warned that pressures inside federal penitentiaries were mounting, and that they were becoming more dangerous and unpredictable. He described a toxic workplace in which the CSC staff often treated each other poorly. One staff member told this writer he was personally threatened by a guard who said, "I should work you over with a baseball bat."

In 2013, the gradual erosion of programming continued, as did the ability of prisoners to earn and keep money. In addition, libraries were being closed or access was being restricted. Prisoner social events that helped in adjusting to the outside world were cancelled. Part-time prison chaplain contracts were not renewed.

The ombudsman was careful to give credit to the CSC where it had shown progress, but a level of frustration with the CSC's resistance to change permeated the 2013–2014 report. The OCI had made recommendations about how better to handle cases of natural-cause deaths in custody. The CSC had rejected them all. The CSC had also done nothing with the OCI's recommendations after Ashley Smith's suicide. Sapers said that this was untenable, unacceptable, and inconsistent with the CSC's responsibility to respond to OCI recommendations. The CSC refused to prohibit long-term segregation of mentally ill prisoners or those at risk of suicide or serious self-injury. Sapers said use of physical restraints, pepper spray, or placements in isolation or observation cells for mentally ill prisoners had become increasingly counterproductive and harmful.

Sapers noted that the cost of keeping each prisoner in the system was $117,778 per year for men and $211,618 for women. He said such an enormous investment should provide more than simple incapacitation. Significantly, he said we need to incarcerate fewer people.

The ombudsman also pointed out occasional anomalies in the use of public funding. In pursuit of the CSC's dogged and futile efforts to remove all drugs from the prisons, it budgeted $266,918 for special toilets designed to permit a more sanitary retrieval of drugs being smuggled by swallowing. The CSC had already invested in ion scanners to detect drugs, even though these are notoriously unreliable, finding false positives at a high rate. This results in visits being curtailed or eliminated.

By the time of his 2014–2015 report, the OCI had finally received the CSC's response to Ashley Smith's suicide (which occurred in 2007). Sapers said it failed to address specific recommendations of the coroner's jury and failed to make a commitment to reforms. And after a three-year wait for the CSC's response to recommendations of his report on assaults on women in secure units, Sapers said it was "particularly disappointing, lacking depth and substance."

By 2014, prisoners were eight to nine times more likely to end their lives than other Canadians. The CSC had been told three years earlier to make cells suicide-proof, but no action had been taken. The CSC continued to put mentally ill, suicidal, and self-harming prisoners in long-term administrative segregation in cells with known "suspension points" (from which they might hang themselves).

Sapers said that such an omission would not be tolerated in any other institutional-care facility, and that the CSC was failing in its duty of care. Alarmingly, the CSC was using administrative segregation as punishment in order to circumvent due-process requirements. Federal prisons were now functioning as psychiatric, palliative, and long-term care facilities — all of which jobs they were not qualified to undertake.

Violent incidents of all kinds were up in 2014. Assaults among prisoners had increased by 17 percent over five years, while incidents of self-harm went up by 56 percent. Use-of-force incidents increased almost 20 percent in one year.

There was a deterioration of other conditions in the prisons — the quality of food declined and there was an elimination of "non-essential" dental care. Likewise, Circles of Support and Accountability were defunded, despite being especially important to rehabilitation, providing counselling to those who had committed sexual assault, and producing a significant *decrease* in reoffending. This was despite a very positive five-year assessment. All of this was happening in an environment in which expenditures on corrections had increased 70 percent in ten years. As well, total costs of the entire criminal justice system were up 25 percent over ten years — ironically, approximately the same percentage as the decrease in the crime rate.

The preceding analyses and statistics refer to the federal prison system. Provincial and territorial prisons are operated according to the differing dictates of each government. These deal with prisoners who are serving sentences of two-years-less-a-day (a "deuce less" in prison jargon) or less, and with remand prisoners. The latter have never been convicted of anything, but are confined to prison while awaiting the disposition of their cases by guilty plea or by trial. They often comprise the majority of prisoners in a system.

Provincial and territorial prisons share all of the problems that federal prisons experience. In addition, they house a particularly volatile population, one made so because of the excessive overcrowding caused by large number of remand prisoners, and because the population is coming and going more quickly due to the shorter sentences. Programming is harder to administer with such a transitory population. Equally significant, within these institutions an exceptionally diverse collection of humanity is incarcerated. Persons accused of every type of crime, from shoplifting to murder, are housed there since they include remand prisoners. This makes for a very dangerous and unpredictable atmosphere. All of the poor conditions described by the preceding analyses are equally present and often heightened in the provincial and territorial systems.

The maintenance of humane conditions is well-nigh impossible within a system of extreme power imbalances where what happens behind closed doors largely stays there. As the OCI points out, corrections is one area of public administration that is far from "open by default." On the contrary, prisons operate far from public scrutiny. If the system is ever to be safe, lawful, and accountable — if that is even possible — this will have to change.

3

PRISON CONDITIONS: NOT FIT FOR MAN OR BEAST

What is the face of the victims of current prison conditions? Here is one story told to me by someone who worked in the Kingston prisons.

Jim's whole family was known to police. Prison was nothing new in his circle. Jim himself was serving a life sentence for killing the person who had stolen his car. He had then settled down in prison to pursue an education and was co-operative, bright, and focused on his studies.

However, Jim was also being regularly "used" by other prisoners for anal sex. It got to the point where he was hospitalized and had to have an operation to fix the damage to his rectum. He was then transferred to another prison where he took a program that was to help him be more assertive. He believed that his circumstances would improve. However, the rapes resumed. Jim finally hanged himself in his cell.

This is just one example of what can happen in a system where there is insufficient care and little control over the violence in prison. Recently, there have been a multitude of shocking incidents, and sometimes these occur at the hands of the keepers. In Ontario, a prisoner who had been placed into the same unit as a rival gang member was badly beaten, suffering permanent brain damage. He sued the government and won. The court found that the authorities were negligent and should have known the likely outcome of placing these two men in the same unit. This habit of "double-dooring," where staff place incompatible prisoners in the same confined space knowing what the likely outcome will be, is all too frequent.

More than forty years ago, Mark MacGuigan issued a warning about the consequences of permitting guards free rein in prisons. The power balance is such that prisoners can be and are exposed to predictable violence on a regular basis. At the Standing Senate Committee on Human Rights in February 2017, Catherine Latimer, executive director of the John Howard Society, described some of the behaviour of staff in the prison system. She said that some practised deliberate cruelty, and that prisoners in maximum security were goaded and disrespected by staff. She also said that some staff encouraged prisoners to kill themselves.

There are other examples of the consequences of poor prison conditions. In the fall of 2016, a prisoner at the Ottawa jail died of the flu. This man was serving his first prison sentence — six months for minor drug offences. He was fifty-nine years old, and had been forced to sleep on the floor of his cell. He had exhibited serious symptoms for many days, but proper care was not provided.

In 2016, the overcrowded Winnipeg Remand Centre reported five deaths in one year. One of these men was in custody because of the minor charge of mischief. After being denied his medications, he died of an epileptic seizure.

But nowhere is the shocking treatment of prisoners more evident than in the overuse of segregation.

A CRISIS IN SEGREGATION

Howard Sapers was recently appointed as Independent Advisor on Corrections Reform to the government of Ontario. His appointment coincided with the sudden glare of publicity resulting from an almost accidental discovery by Renu Mandhane, the chief commissioner of the Ontario Human Rights Commission, in 2016. She was informed by a guard at the Thunder Bay Correctional Centre that Adam Capay had spent four years in continuous segregation while waiting for his trial on a murder charge.

This prisoner was being housed in a windowless cell where the lights were on twenty-four hours a day. The cell was lined with Plexiglas. The commissioner met with Adam. She reported that he had difficulty speaking, perhaps because of the lack of human contact, that he could not tell day from night, and that he had self-harmed. Like Ashley Smith, Adam Capay originally went to prison for something relatively innocuous. He used a baseball bat to smash his mother's car. Although no one was hurt in that incident, he was charged with using a weapon. The murder charge arose from an altercation in the prison that resulted in the death of another prisoner. Media attention to the case of Adam Capay has been unrelenting and has led to serious questions about how the provincial system operates.

Eight years earlier (2008), another aboriginal prisoner, Christopher Coaster, died of dehydration in the same cell that later housed Capay. Mr. Coaster was suffering from alcohol withdrawal. It was a particularly hot summer, there was no air conditioning or fan, and, as was the case later with Adam Capay, the cell was covered with Plexiglas, making it like an oven. Before he died, Mr. Coaster was hallucinating, banging himself against the walls, laughing hysterically, bruising himself, and taking no food or drink. How is this possible in Canada in the twenty-first century?

Although international standards say that more than fifteen consecutive days in segregation amounts to torture, Canadian prisons surpass this on a regular basis, using segregation as an administrative tool. There is no limit on how much time a prisoner can be held in "administrative solitary confinement." And it is often used on the most vulnerable prisoners.

All recommendations to curtail the use of segregation in the federal system were in vain until the past two years, when there was a sudden reduction in its use by about half. A year ago, when the new Liberal government was sworn in, the prime minister's mandate letter to the minister of justice and attorney general instructed her to set a cap of fifteen days for segregation, in accordance with international standards. The guards' union has warned that this will jeopardize safety in the institution, but statistics do not bear this out. There has been no increase in violence since the sudden decline in use beginning in 2013–2014, and use-of-force incidents have barely increased.

Yet the use of this damaging form of control is still very high. What does it actually mean to be in the "hole" for an extended period of time? An expert on segregation, Michael

Jackson has written extensively about the damage it does, and the many concerted efforts made by governments and other organizations to curtail it. Jackson talks about his clients in the 1970s begging and pleading to be let out of solitary. Prisoners set themselves on fire in their cells in an effort to get out or die. They descended into total insanity. Prisoners who were well-respected "stand-up cons" were screaming and banging their heads against steel doors and concrete walls. They often took their own lives. The CSC refused to act on recommendations and advice from numerous official sources.

If there was ever a reason to act on the issue of overuse of segregation, it was the suicide of nineteen-year-old Ashley Smith in 2007. I have already recounted Ashley's four years of agony as she travelled through the prison system. In the end, Ashley was placed in an isolation cell with no stimulation at all available to her — not even a book or piece of paper to write on. The cell measured six feet by nine feet. There was no mattress. There are shocking photographs of her trussed up and restrained. The CSC knew that she had been in isolation for long periods of time and that it was highly detrimental to her health, both mental and physical. However, the authorities did nothing for her. She finally choked herself to death while seven staff members watched. They had previously been ordered not to go to her aid until Ashley had stopped breathing. This also happened in Canada in the twenty-first century.

Another suicide in segregation that galvanized the press and shone a light on the federal system was that of Eddie Snowshoe, who died in the Edmonton maximum-security institution in 2010. The official 2014 report on his death showed that he had attempted suicide on four previous occasions. When he succeeded, he had been in segregation for 162 days. Although he was healthy when he first arrived in prison, he developed mental illness over his three years in custody.

Senator Kim Pate is former executive director of the Canadian Association of Elizabeth Fry Societies, which advocates for marginalized, victimized, and institutionalized women and girls throughout Canada. She says that since the suicide of Ashley Smith, she has been seeing an increased use of force against female prisoners who have mental health problems, or are apt to self-harm, or both. It seems that no lessons have been learned. In fact, in June of 2016, Terry Baker died at the same institution as Ashley Smith (Grand Valley in Ontario) and by the same means (a ligature around her neck).

The Central East Correctional Centre in Lindsay, Ontario, a superjail with capacity to house 1,184 prisoners, also recently reported a death in segregation. The prisoner was thirty years old and schizophrenic. He was allowed no visits, was restrained physically and pepper-sprayed, and wore a spit hood (to prevent him from spitting on staff). When he died, he was badly bruised and had a large gash on his forehead. Some staff were suspended after this death, and the guards' union said they needed more training to deal with mental illness.

Prisoners are beginning to resort to the courts to fight the use of segregation. Recently, three aboriginal prisoners at Edmonton Institution managed to obtain an order to be removed from the "hole" after arguing their case in Alberta's Court of Queen's Bench. Their spokesperson, Matthew Hamm, has serious mental issues, but is high-functioning. He filed a *habeas corpus* application without assistance, alleging that the institution had denied the three of them medications for their illnesses, and had denied them access to aboriginal spiritual practices. As well, the charges against all three were shown to be groundless. They had been in the "hole" for six weeks. The judgement releasing them from segregation was scathing in its comments about the Institution's behaviour.

Significantly, the moment Mr. Hamm and his friends filed the motion for release, their lives in the prison became harder. Guards released maggots in Mr. Hamm's cell. His court filings were held up at the prison. Five days before the hearing, guards took away his clothing, gave him a smock to wear, and placed him on suicide watch. Mr. Hamm said that nothing he had done justified this response. Sometime after the success of their lawsuit, one of the others, Shawn Keepness, was shot in the testicles by a guard using a rubber bullet. Mr. Keepness believes that this also was retribution.

In its reply to Mr. Hamm's litigation, the CSC claimed that it does not use solitary confinement, but does use "administrative segregation," which they say is more humane because some visits are allowed. The "visits" referred to are the perfunctory calls of medical staff and personnel. The CSC also claimed, in the face of massive evidence to the contrary, that there are no negative health effects of living in segregation.

In an unprecedented move, the College of Family Physicians of Canada, representing about thirty-five thousand doctors, called for an all-out ban on segregation in 2017. In doing so, they emphasized that the use of solitary confinement can have a negative impact on a person's health and worsen pre-existing conditions, especially for youth and those who are mentally ill. Their move follows recent developments in the use of administrative segregation. The CSC has released new draft rules that will make minor changes. Prisoners will be allowed to spend two hours outside their cells instead of one. They will have immediate access to personal property related to hygiene, religion, and medical care. There will be a prohibition on using segregation for significantly impaired mentally ill prisoners, and for those who self-harm, are suicidal, pregnant, physically disabled, or terminally ill.

There are significant problems with these supposed solutions. First, these are proposed changes to CSC rules, and will not be enshrined in legislation. Rules can be and often are changed at will. Second, no limits at all in the number of days that a prisoner can be kept in segregation are contemplated. Third, and perhaps most important, the CSC is still not prepared to accept independent oversight of segregation, as so often requested by the OCI and other advocates.

In June 2017, the federal government tabled legislation that purports to bring the use of segregation into compliance with the Canadian *Charter*. This was done as a last-ditch effort to delay litigation initiated by the British Columbia Civil Liberties Association and the John Howard Society of Canada. The new law would limit the use of segregation to twenty-one consecutive days, to be reduced to fifteen days eighteen months after the bill's passage. However, these caps can still be overridden by the prison warden, and a new independent external review process would have no power to order the release of prisoners held beyond those caps. Experts thus argued that the proposed legislation changes nothing and a British Columbia judge has agreed to allow the litigation to proceed.

Meanwhile, on the advice of former OCI ombudsman Howard Sapers, the Ontario government has just announced that there will be new legislation in the fall of 2017 reflecting changes recommended in his report. Ontario will ban the use of segregation for pregnant women and for the mentally ill, but it is not certain that the province will impose hard caps on the length of time one can spend in segregation. The new minister, a former social worker who has some understanding of the underlying socio-economic factors that contribute to wrongdoing, is determined to do corrections differently. She wants Ontario to become an international model for humane corrections practices. Among other things, she intends to provide greater access for prisoners to books, TVs, radios, playing cards, and fresh air. This is only a beginning, but if her actions follow through on the rhetoric, then Ontario's correctional system is in for a serious overhaul.

VIOLENCE IN PRISON

Violence in the prison system is pervasive, and exposure to it is thought of as one of the prices people pay for breaking the law. Some of the violence is beyond appalling. It may consist of a "tune-up" or beating; it may be a special kind of gang rape, labelled "taking it dry," designed to inflict maximum pain; or it may be murder. The general acceptance of violence as part of the prison experience is now being questioned, as courts are beginning to intervene in cases where it is felt the institution is not doing its job.

Provincial prison authorities came under scrutiny in a recent case. The judge dismissed a charge of assault with a weapon against a prisoner, Michael Short, who was attacked in the Toronto East Detention Centre by someone who believed Short belonged to a rival gang. Short defended himself with a home-made knife or shiv.

Judge Ed Morgan condemned the conditions of incarceration that put prisoners in this position. He said the system could not blame Mr. Short for defending himself as best he could. The reality is, prisoners cannot rely upon the guards to protect them. The only alternative to self-defence, therefore, appears to be a trip to the hospital or the morgue.

The judge laid blame for the incident directly at the feet of the institution. He noted that the guards took a surprisingly long time to respond to a serious incident and then did so in a lackadaisical manner. The guards, on the other hand, say that they want to do a good job, but that they are short-staffed and the facilities are overcrowded. For them to wade into such an incident without sufficient backup would be foolhardy.

Jason Godin, president of the guards' union (the Union of Canadian Correctional Officers, or UCCO), says that working in the prisons is more dangerous now than it was under the restorative justice model espoused by former commissioner of the CSC, Ole Ingstrup, in the 1990s. Godin lays this change at the feet of the tough-on-crime Conservative government, saying he has never seen a more dangerous politician than Prime Minister Stephen Harper.

Violence in prisons comes as no surprise to those of us who have worked in them. In my own experience, prisoners have been attacked or murdered for many reasons — taking someone else's chair in the common room, refusing to "share" drugs, refusing to make visitors smuggle drugs into the prison, being suspected of acting as a snitch or rat, owing a debt, looking into someone's eyes, asking another prisoner what offence they committed: the list goes on — don't *ever* whistle, do be polite, don't reach across someone's plate at meals, don't talk back, and don't whine.

For many prisoners, the best advice is to "do your own time," make no friends, "dummy up," and speak to no one unless asked a direct question. In fact, this strategy of self-isolation often results in prisoners deciding to stay in their "drum" or "house" as much as possible.

One avoidance mechanism is as horrific as the violence a prisoner is seeking to avoid. A new prisoner can obtain protection from another in return for sexual services. He becomes a "kid." As such, however, he can also be "rented out" by his protector to other prisoners. As awful as such a fate is, at least it helps to keep the prisoner alive. Prisoners who do not obtain such "protection" or who break the prisoners' code in some other fashion often meet a brutal fate.

In one case, a prisoner was murdered in the Special Handling Unit (SHU — the "Shoe") at Millhaven Institution. Michael and another prisoner had been charged with the murder. Michael did not do the killing, but he knew who did. Nonetheless, he was now facing a life sentence for murder, charged with helping the killer — an accusation he denied. If he were to finger the "other party" — the person with the shank — he would be known as a rat and would face death at the hands of other prisoners.

Michael did take the witness stand and described what happened, but refused to tell the court who the guilty party was. The judge certainly understood what the stakes were for Michael, but the jury apparently did not. He was convicted of first-degree murder and received a mandatory life sentence with no chance of parole for twenty-five years.

Several months later, the local news reported that yet another prisoner in the SHU had been murdered. Michael had failed to come back from the yard. His strangled body was found under one of the surveillance towers where there were no sight lines. He paid the price of giving evidence for the Crown, even though he had been scrupulous about refusing to name the perpetrator. Some time later, a number of prisoners who had been in the yard at the time of the murder were convicted of his murder. And so the system of violence continues.

In 2014, the federal guards' union president, Kevin Grabowsky, who had thirty-five years' experience at the CSC, said he had never seen the level or intensity of violence that was occurring then. Guards said that rehabilitation programs were taking a back seat to the tough-on-crime agenda, as was health care. They emphasized that most of the prisoners would eventually be released and would be living in our neighbourhoods. The current failure to provide rehabilitation is not good for public safety.

The last decade (2006–2007 to 2014–2015) has seen an increase of 93 percent in violent incidents in the federal system. At Prince Albert Penitentiary, for example, there was a full-scale riot in which one prisoner died. It was reported that the riot might have been ignited by a continuing complaint about meal portion sizes. The Conservative government had decreed that all portions should be the same, regardless of age or activity level.

There is, however, a glimmer of hope since the change of government in 2015, as people anticipate a return to less confrontational corrections.

THE DANGERS OF OVERCROWDING AND LOCKDOWNS

Overcrowding continues to emerge as a cause of considerable discomfort and violence. About halfway through the tough-on-crime decade, guards' unions were complaining about the extent of the problem. They said that nearly 30 percent of prison cells now housed two prisoners and that it was hard to be sure if two prisoners were "compatible": that is, could safely share a cell. Some had previous history together; some belonged to rival gangs; some were vulnerable because they were rapists, child molesters, "rats," or police officers. If the complete file did not follow every prisoner, then mistakes could be made, with serious or fatal consequences. As well, as earlier noted, guards have on occasion been complicit in putting prisoners' lives at risk by ignoring available information that shows an incompatibility.

Guards have also complained that new minimum sentences mean there is no incentive for prisoners to work toward their release by taking rehabilitative programs. More people are being sent to penitentiaries; of those, more are staying longer and more are being kept at higher security levels. As well, there are high percentages who are suffering from mental illness, drug dependency, or both. It is easy to see how volatile the situation of housing more than one prisoner in a tiny cell, with one or both sometimes sleeping on mattresses on the floor, can become. The atmosphere of overcrowded prisons also becomes noisy and chaotic, and diseases spread like wildfire.

Despite all of the problems associated with overcrowding, then public safety minister Vic Toews responded by changing the rules, to allow for double-bunking as the new normal. He insisted that overcrowding was not a significant contributor to violence. Howard Sapers said it was neither safe nor humane, and that it was inconsistent with our international obligations under the United Nations Standard Minimum Rules for the Treatment of Prisoners, endorsed by Canada in 1975. Nevertheless, double-bunking increased by 50 percent between 2005 and 2010.

The auditor general (AG) reported on overcrowding in federal prisons in 2014, saying that even the 2,700 new cells the CSC was building would not be sufficient to accommodate the expected increase in numbers of prisoners over the next few years. The AG said that prisoners were even being crowded into segregation cells and into cells smaller than five square metres. He confirmed that this produced safety issues for both staff and prisoners.

Overcrowding also has consequences for public safety, given that prisoners are being released from high-security settings directly to the street more often. If there is no room in medium- and minimum-security institutions, then it becomes impossible to "cascade" maximum-security prisoners down through the system gradually. The point of cascading is that when prisoners are finally released from minimum-security settings, they are used to more freedom and responsibility and are better prepared for life on the street.

The AG has also noted that prisoners — especially aboriginal prisoners — are being released without proper rehabilitation programs, and are going directly to the street from maximum- and medium-security institutions. When any prisoner is released unprepared for living in society, it does not bode well for public safety.

Catherine Latimer, executive director of the John Howard Society, reports that, lately, increasing numbers of former prisoners are returning to prison for violent offences within five years of completing their sentences. Evidence would suggest that this is likely one result of the harsher climate produced by a tough-on-crime philosophy. Latimer says that our prisons are now in crisis. Canada's recent prison policies have recently drawn international criticism, with the United Nations calling upon us to reduce overcrowding, limit solitary confinement, and improve health care for the mentally ill.

In provincial prisons, the issue of overcrowding is especially serious. About two-thirds of the prisoners in the provincial systems are on remand — almost double the number in 1996. Remand prisoners are those who are waiting for their trial date and have not been convicted of anything. They are often in custody only because they are unable to meet the conditions of their bail order. That is, a judge has found them to be appropriate candidates for release on bail (not a flight risk and not a danger to the public), but they are not able to produce the required surety or cash bail.

The old Don Jail in Toronto was particularly notorious as a remand centre. I was a regular visitor and the place would have driven me to desperate measures in a very short time. The facility itself was ancient, falling apart, and far from adequate to house the large number of prisoners. Men lounged and slept on the floor in the corridors on mattresses. There was an extreme level of noise, as the younger prisoners blasted music as loud as possible. Many older prisoners were at the end of their tether, unable to tolerate the behaviour of the "young punks." The friction often broke out into physical altercations. Little wonder that guards were known to smuggle marijuana into the jail at times so that the prisoners would "mellow out." It was a hell-hole, and no one was sorry when it was closed. Unfortunately, the Don was replaced by a "superjail" — the Toronto South Detention Centre — where the problems continue, but on a larger scale.

These overcrowded conditions should soon be alleviated because of the Supreme Court decision in *R. v. Jordan*. In that case, the court set down limits for the length of time it takes to get a remand prisoner to trial — from eighteen to thirty months, depending on the type of charge. This means that the criminal justice system will be compelled to move remand prisoners through the process much more quickly, which should sharply reduce the numbers in provincial prisons.

In remand, everyone is housed together, regardless of mental vulnerability, drug dependency, or tendency to violent behaviour. The same is true for the "bull pen," where prisoners are all caged together when they come to court. If a prisoner happens to end up there with a sworn enemy, violence is predictable. The transportation that moves prisoners from place to place is also a place where, since prisoners of all types are thrown together, problems often occur. Everybody sits in the back of the paddy wagon, completely exposed to one another for the duration of the trip. Extreme violence is often the result, and it is not always perpetrated by the prisoners. Police officers who are in charge of transporting prisoners sometimes openly brag about how they take the corners really fast and hit the brakes as hard as they can. Prisoners who are shackled at the legs and wrists, but with no seat belts or other protection, frequently emerge from the vans covered in bruises and blood.

Lockdowns have recently increased in provincial prisons, and add to the misery and danger. There were nine hundred lockdowns in Ontario in 2015, more than triple the number in 2009. These lead to frustration in both prisoners and staff. Prisoners are confined to their cells, often with two or more others. They do not normally have access to showers, dining areas, fresh air, programs, or visits.

During one lockdown, a prisoner reported sleeping on the floor between two beds in a cell that measured seven by two metres. His head rested beside the toilet. People stepped on him on their way to the toilet and splashed him with their urine. He had to eat his meals on the floor as well. When disputes arose, there was nowhere to go to cool off. As he put it, if there are two people in a cell, one can go to the door and calm down. If there are three, there is nowhere to go. Some prisons have even housed individuals in the admitting and discharge area (London), or in the shower area (Ottawa).

As a result of the tension lockdowns produce, assaults by prisoners on guards have climbed, going from 324 in 2009 to 524 in 2013. In the Toronto South Detention Centre, for example, lockdowns are frequent. Prisoners are sometimes kept in their cells for twenty-four hours a day for several days in a row. Guards blame understaffing in the face of increasing numbers of prisoners. Toronto South opened in 2014 and was immediately reporting high rates of assault by prisoners on each other and on guards. Conditions in the $1.1 billion facility are so bad that there have been prisoner strikes, riots, and many lockdowns. The institution blamed this on understaffing, so the ministry promised two thousand new hires. There have been 229 hires in the past three or four years, but this is not nearly enough. The number of lockdown days has increased from 181 in 2015 (a low estimate, as the data include only days locked down because of staff shortages) to 243 in 2016. In October 2016, a superior court judge said the facility was in crisis.

It is clear that these dangerous conditions have been exacerbated by government policy over the past decade. Howard Sapers in his final OCI report criticized what he called mass incarceration, arbitrary and abusive conditions of detention, and even the so-called victims' rights agenda that was at the centre of the Conservative program. He says that when he talks to Canadians he finds they want safety, and they express Canadian values of compassion, not vengeance.

Sapers described the current system as "punishment with no apparent limits." Retribution and reprisal reign supreme. Prisoners are made to pay and pay again for their mistakes. He said the tough-on-crime approach is making prisons more austere, crowded, and unsafe, and less effective. He again compared present-day conditions to those that caused Kingston Penitentiary to blow up forty-six years ago.

ABORIGINAL PRISONERS

Over the past few years, the number of aboriginal and minority prisoners has grown, far out of proportion to their numbers in the Canadian population. These prisoners are more likely to be in maximum-security prisons and in segregation. They are more likely to be the subject of use-of-force interventions. They incur more disciplinary charges. They are released much later in their sentences, are less likely to be granted day or full parole, and are far more likely to be detained to their warrant expiry dates. They are also more likely to have their parole revoked for technicalities.

As mentioned earlier, in January 2016, 25 percent of the prisoner population in the federal correctional system was aboriginal. For women, the percentage was 35 percent. Between 2005 and 2015, the number of federal prisoners grew by 10 percent but it grew by more than 50 percent for aboriginal men and more than double for aboriginal women. The proportion of aboriginal people in Canada is only 4.3 percent.

Aboriginal prisoners in the federal system are younger, less educated, and more likely to suffer from drug dependency and mental health problems than other prisoners. Two-thirds of their parents have abused drugs, and 48 percent have at one time been removed from the family home. Almost all of the women have experienced traumatic events like sexual and physical abuse and drug abuse.

When the Prison for Women was closed down, the plan was to improve conditions for women prisoners, including aboriginal women, by placing them in locations closer to their homes. There are now five women's penitentiaries and a number of healing lodges, but there has been an alarming increase in the numbers of aboriginal women in the system. It is thought that judges feel justified in sending women to these facilities rather than finding alternatives to incarceration, because the new institutions are supposed to provide programs that will help with rehabilitation. They are also somewhat closer to the women's homes; but ease of access has not really been provided, and it is still very hard for families and friends to visit.

I will be talking later about small, local prisons in countries like Norway, where this model appears to be successful at helping prisoners maintain their family and community connections, thus enabling their rehabilitation. The lower recidivism rates for such prisons are notable. Why this model appears not to be working as well in Canada is a matter for discussion. It may be that our vast geography militates against our ability to provide truly local institutions — close to prisoners' homes. Almost certainly, Norwegian families have more resources to pay for the trip to a prison than do average aboriginal families. Or it may be that the Canadian institutions do not provide the same range of programs that the Scandinavian ones do, thus failing to provide the rehabilitation that might help reduce recidivism. Why our new system is not working remains an open question, but what we do know is that the decentralization of federal imprisonment of aboriginal women in Canada has not succeeded in the way we hoped.

In fact, those who work with this population suggest that these new women's prisons represent a continuation of the harm created by residential schools. Children are removed from their mothers as a matter of course. There is little chance of prisoners getting their children back. There are few visitors because the prisons are in remote locations. The healing lodge at Maple Creek, Saskatchewan, has such a poor road in that it is necessary to travel there by truck.

There is little or no acknowledgement in these facilities of the aboriginal way of doing justice — no healing circles, no community effort. Elders may come in to conduct sweat lodges, but the prisoners remain in their cells. In sum, these prisons are European constructs that do not speak to the aboriginal way of life. They appear to merely warehouse mainly non-violent women at enormous cost, causing untold damage to them, their families, and their communities. And their number continue to grow.

According to the OCI, the social history considerations required for aboriginal people under the *Gladue* decision of the Supreme Court of Canada are not being properly employed in the correctional setting. *Gladue* requires that special attention be paid to the circumstances of aboriginal people, including histories of discrimination, abuse, dislocation, substance abuse, and so on, and that the aboriginal heritage or connection of these prisoners be considered. (The *Gladue* case will be examined in detail when I talk about alternative approaches to justice.) As well, aboriginal cultural advisors — elders — are not being used as required. The number of hearings that include elders is now the lowest in the past ten years. The CSC has still not appointed a deputy commissioner for aboriginal offenders, as repeatedly recommended by the OCI.

The CSC cannot control who gets sent to its prisons or how many. These are decisions for the courts. But the racist aspects of how these prisoners have to serve their time deserve special attention. Conditions of incarceration reflect to a large degree the discrimination experienced by aboriginal people outside prison.

REFUGEES

Canada has come under fire internationally for its treatment of asylum seekers or refugees. Those who are detained because they have insufficient documents or for other reasons are housed in three medium-security detention centres or in maximum-security provincial prisons. The average stay is three weeks, but hundreds stay much longer and some have been incarcerated for as long as seven years.

Unlike virtually every other Western country, Canada has no limit at all on the length of time someone can be kept in detention. The EU's limit is eighteen months, while other countries have to release their detainees within ninety days if they are unable to deport them. Federal government lawyers were arguing as recently as May 2017 that indefinite detention is necessary to ensure public safety. Yet some detainees have been in custody for years without any convictions or even criminal charges.

There is an automatic thirty-day review, but there is no actual due process and the reviews are described by lawyers as "Kafkaesque." If a detainee has failed to be released after six months, his or her chances of ever being released fall to 1 percent. Meantime, detainees are treated for all intents and purposes as if they are criminals.

Children are treated like adults. They have no rights at all — no right to a review or anything else. They are searched regularly and allowed outside only for one hour per day, just like the adults. There is severe psychological distress for all, but particularly for children.

In 2015–2016, there were 6,596 refugees detained in Canada, including 201 children. Of those refugees incarcerated, in January 2016, two-thirds were housed in maximum-security provincial prisons, even though the available immigration centres were not full. In August 2016 the government announced $138 million for the expansion of immigration centres to reduce the use of prisons, but nothing has so far changed.

The current federal government has restored the health care funding for refugees that had been removed by the previous Conservative government, and has promised additional health care funding. It is past time that Liberals also take seriously United Nations and Red Cross criticisms and stop detaining asylum seekers and refugees indefinitely and stop treating them like criminals. It costs $250 per day — about $90,000 per year — to house each person detained. Advocates say alternatives are available — community shelters, reporting requirements, and supervision arrangements would be more than adequate. If the authorities are not convinced by compassion and simple decency, perhaps the financial implications will move them to action.

PRISONERS SUFFERING FROM MENTAL ILLNESS AND DRUG ABUSE

Mental illness and drug abuse have emerged as serious concerns involving large numbers of prisoners, and the numbers are rising. The prison ombudsman has repeatedly called for more treatment facilities and more expertise in dealing with these problems, but concerns continue to grow. Mental health issues are two to three times more common in prison than outside. Almost half of incoming male prisoners have drug abuse problems (alcohol, or drugs, or both) and over one-third have concurrent disorders. Psychotropic drugs are prescribed for 30 percent of prisoners, compared to 8 percent of the Canadian population. Fifty percent more women prisoners than men receive these medications.

In 2015, after four years of recommendations by the OCI that the CSC develop a reliable system to diagnose FASD (fetal alcohol spectrum disorder), there was still no such system in place. Without a way of diagnosing the disorder, there is no way to provide treatment to those who need it.

Self-harm incidents in the federal system have tripled in the last decade. Self-harm is a coping mechanism whereby prisoners find a release from uncontrollable anxiety by cutting, head-banging, or using ligatures. These activities release endorphins into the brain and tend to calm the person. Such behaviour is not necessarily suicidal, but the CSC's response is to isolate the prisoner (essentially, to use segregation), which can increase the risk of suicide.

The rising number of mentally ill prisoners has resulted in the CSC requiring at least five hundred acute psychiatric care beds and nearly one thousand intermediate beds. The OCI reports that to create the intermediate beds, the CSC closed two-thirds of its existing psychiatric beds.

There is considerable evidence that prisons have become the default destination for those with mental illness (as they are for those who use certain drugs). Resources for mentally ill people on the outside are stretched, and there appear to be no more dollars for health care. Not treating people who have a mental illness can result in their acting in ways that are illegal. As a result, people often fear this portion of the population — even though violent crime by the mentally ill is uncommon.

The recent exceptional example of Vincent Li shows the implications of lack of treatment and of public prejudice against those with mental illness. Li, whose recent release from custody has caused consternation among the public, killed a young man on a Greyhound bus in Manitoba in 2008. The details were horrific. An undiagnosed schizophrenic at the time, Li explained that he had heard voices telling him to save people from an alien attack. He was found to be "not criminally responsible" and sent to live in a psychiatric facility. There he was diagnosed and treated with medication. In 2017, he was adjudged to be safe to live without conditions in the community.

Although much outrage has been expressed as a result of this decision, and although the family of the victim is opposed to his release, it is hard to argue that this was not the right decision. In our hyper-risk-averse world, Li's psychiatrists would not have recommended release if there were any danger to the public. Li himself has no reason to stop taking his medication. This decision was a triumph of good sense over the fearmongering that has directed criminal justice policy for some years. It is a sign that we are capable of dealing with mental illness in a compassionate and sensible way without jeopardizing public safety.

Li was successfully treated in a psychiatric institution. However, most of those convicted of a crime, who suffer from mental illness, are not sent to such institutions; instead, they are sent to prison. This compounds the problem because incarcerating mentally ill people exacerbates mental illness, and it may also cause mental illness in people who have shown no signs of problems before entering prison.

Remand prisoners are among the sickest in the country, but for them there is no treatment at all. Everyone seems to agree that there need to be more forensic beds for the mentally ill, but resources have not been forthcoming.

In the wake of the "deinstitutionalization" of the mentally ill some years ago, few resources were targeted to assist these patients to live in the community. As a result, many fell afoul of the law. And although there have been some efforts to divert mentally ill people away from the prison system by means of mental-health courts, these courts are few and far between. Such courts operate much like drug-treatment courts, taking accused persons out of the traditional court setting and making an effort to set up a treatment program that will keep them out of prison. But again, there are few of these courts, so jails and prisons have become the new asylums.

Not only do prisons pose a serious threat to the mental health of prisoners, they also pose problems for their physical health. They are at serious risk of injury or worse when they live in a prison population. I defended a client on an attempted murder charge that involved the serious injury of two prisoners housed in the SHU at Millhaven. As I have said previously, this unit was like no other and seemed to operate on a knife edge at all times; the relationship between guards and prisoners was either non-existent or very ugly. In fact, there was virtually no direct contact between them. When I was interviewing prisoners in this unit, there were no guards within my sight except for dark shadows moving behind a bubble of black glass over my shoulder. Everything in the unit was controlled electronically. The guards and prisoners had as little to do with each other as possible. As a result, the unit was essentially being run by the prisoners themselves in an atmosphere of tension and fear. Anything creating friction or irritation could result in serious incidents, up to and including riots and murder.

Into this brittle and nerve-wracking atmosphere, the authorities decided to place two new prisoners, both of them with serious mental illnesses. They had habits that were extremely upsetting to the other prisoners. One of them, for example, had an uncontrollable urge to masturbate whenever he saw a female. This caused problems for the female nurses, who were among the few staff who had close contact with the prisoners. This habit was also more than a mere annoyance for other prisoners.

The presence of these two men destroyed the balance in the unit. Under the system of authority that quietly existed in the SHU population, word came down that these two prisoners had to be transferred out, or eliminated. Since the prisoners had no power to move them, the solution was obvious. A prisoner from the unit gave evidence that he had wielded the knife, and he explained why to the jury. Both co-accused were acquitted. No one else was ever prosecuted for the crime.

Another recent case drew attention again to the dangers of housing mentally ill prisoners in the general population. A schizophrenic street person, Jeffrey Munro, was living on a range in the Don Jail. He had been arrested for allegedly exposing himself in public. In the Don, he was of course living with all kinds of people, ranging from those on remand for murder all the way down to petty thieves. He did not fit in. After an altercation with another prisoner over a stolen bag of potato chips, Jeffrey Munro was killed.

Guards, too, are affected by these conditions. They work in a dangerous and emotionally corrosive atmosphere, according to a recent Department of Public Safety report. Thirty-six percent of male federal prison guards suffer from post-traumatic stress disorder (PTSD), as compared to 9 percent of the military returning from tours in Afghanistan. This is a result of having to deal with a great number of high-stress scenarios: prison gangs, suicides, medical emergencies, makeshift weapons, fires, attacks, plots. The health ministries of Ontario and Manitoba have now recognized prison guards as "first responders," meaning that they now get treatment for PTSD immediately approved.

This is important on a number of levels, if we consider that guards are the people who oversee the safety and well-being of prisoners. How well-equipped can they be to do this job if they are suffering from the symptoms of PTSD themselves — irritability, emotional swings, occasional violent outbursts, and so on? The combination of these symptoms with the multiple syndromes and problems experienced by prisoners creates a toxic mix. It makes prisons far from ideal as places to "correct" wrongdoers.

PHYSICAL HEALTH OF PRISONERS

Physical health care has also emerged as an area of serious concern in prison. As noted, prisons are required to provide the same access to health care as for the rest of us, but they must do so from their own operating budgets. International rules — the United Nations Standard Minimum Rules of the Treatment of Prisoners (the Mandela Rules) — say that health care is to be provided by agencies that are ordinarily responsible for health. It is not to be provided by systems that are specifically responsible for prisons. Only three provinces in Canada can claim to adhere to this rule — Nova Scotia, Alberta, and British Columbia. Otherwise, Canada falls woefully short of this international standard.

Jurisdictions where provinces do provide the care boast lower recidivism rates, greater participation in studies, and better treatment of tuberculosis, HIV, hepatitis C, and sexually transmitted diseases. Ninety percent of the federal prison population suffers from a diagnosable illness, with one-half displaying antisocial personality disorder, so providing the best of care is essential to better results in the short and long term.

In 2016, Howard Sapers said that in nine of the ten past years health care was the subject of the most complaints received by his office. He also noted that deaths in prison are often not treated with compassion. In one case, when a family member travelled to the prison to view his deceased relative, he was told the prisoner had already been cremated. Some time later, the ashes were sent to his house by Purolator. More recently, the family of a deceased prisoner had to come up with $800 to retrieve his body from the Montreal airport.

Many terminally ill prisoners are refused permission for compassionate release so they can die surrounded by their family members, a right that is routinely extended to prisoners in other countries. In 2014–2015, the Parole Board of Canada received twenty-eight requests for the Royal Prerogative of Mercy. None was granted.

About a quarter of the federal prison population are over the age of fifty. A full 20 percent are lifers. People who go into the system are often already sicker or more prone to disease than the general population. Conditions in prison can exacerbate these problems. And another issue has recently arisen. Now that assisted dying is legal in Canada, many are asking whether or not it will be made available to prisoners on the same basis that it is available to other Canadians.

Health care for prisoners should be cause for concern for everyone, since prisoners released into the community can spread disease, and will also rely heavily on the health care system if they emerge from prison unhealthy. The prison ombudsman has repeatedly asked the CSC to consider harm-reduction measures to reduce the spread of blood-borne diseases like HIV/AIDS and hepatitis C through the sharing of needles. As he pointed out, prison needle exchange programs have been implemented in prisons throughout the world, starting in Switzerland twenty years ago. Even Iran has one. These programs have succeeded in reducing the spread of such diseases. As well, the number of drug abusers who seek treatment for their dependencies increases when there are needle exchanges, and the need for health interventions related to overdose incidents decreases.

Not only is a provision of a needle exchange important, however, so too is education of prisoners about the importance of this, since prisoners are often ignorant of the dangers of sharing needles. One prisoner apparently believed that sharing a tattooing needle was perfectly safe as long as the needle had been exposed to direct sunlight for twenty-four hours. Evidence shows that needle exchanges and safe tattooing programs reduce the transmission of blood-borne disease, and do so without jeopardizing the safety of staff or prisoners. However, the CSC has not only refused to institute harm-reduction programs, but has also terminated a pilot program for safe tattooing.

Dental care is another challenge. The CSC shows a cavalier attitude toward the provision of this health service. In 2014, the CSC reduced its budget for dental services by $2 million. This represented a reduction of 30 percent over two years. Federal prisoners now receive an oral exam and treatment plan once every five years rather than every year. Those in remote locations receive no care at all. Some can gain access to dental care only if they receive an Escorted Temporary Absence pass, which is not easily available. Many prisoners need dental care more than most of the Canadian population.

According to Kim Pate, security concerns and the way prisons are managed often mean medications are unavailable or are arbitrarily changed by prisons. Access to medical services may be limited, resulting in illnesses not being diagnosed in a reasonable time, and such chronic diseases as diabetes not being managed with the care they would receive in the community, resulting in serious complications.

Standards of care vary widely from province to province in the provincial prison system. For example, Nova Scotia has on-site nursing seven days a week, but only from 8 a.m. to 8 p.m. A prisoner recently died because he apparently overdosed at an inconvenient time. In Saskatchewan, by contrast, prison nurses are available for sixteen hours a day. Doctors also offer weekly clinics and are otherwise on call.

In 2014, nursing hours in federal prisons were cut across the board. For example, the Prairie region has gone from twenty-four-hour-a-day nursing to just eight or twelve hours. The CSC says the reductions are "cost neutral." The Professional Institute of the Public Service of Canada, however, called these kinds of changes very significant. They will be harmful for nurses, prison guards, and prisoners alike. Nurses are worried about the increased pressure of restricted hours, and wonder who will do the job on late-night shifts. Medications, for example, should not be administered by unqualified staff. Yet it will probably be guards who will have to do this job. The guards' union is very uncomfortable with this. They say around-the-clock nursing care is essential.

The new Toronto South Detention Centre has produced some horror stories on the health care front. One prisoner, age forty-eight, has spent a total of seventeen years in various prisons and jails. He has mental health issues, is a crack user, and was born with an imperforate anus. This means that he cannot have a proper bowel movement without certain medical supplies, and these have to be provided on schedule. On one occasion, he was left sitting in soiled underwear for more than three days in segregation waiting for his supplies and some clean clothes. He gets very sick if he can't self-administer the saline solution that enables his system to operate, and he does not eat in the meantime.

Also at Toronto East, a prisoner spent 103 days in segregation because he required the use of a walker, but walkers are deemed to be contraband in the general population.

Newly released prisoners continue to suffer the consequences of poor care in prison. Overdose deaths, mainly related to opioid dependency, are alarmingly common among this group. In Ontario, for example, methadone treatment of drug dependency is not readily available in provincial institutions. Thus, if when drug abusers are released they return to drug use after a period of abstention in prison, they are at high risk for overdose. This is because their systems are no longer able to tolerate their normal dose of a drug. They take an amount that they think should be safe for them, only to find that it is not.

Significantly, one in ten people who died of an overdose in Ontario over a period of seven years had been released from prison within the past twelve months. In the face of this evidence, the provincial health minister ordered the prisons to immediately begin distributing naloxone (the antidote to opioid overdoses) to newly released prisoners. He had to overrule his own bureaucrats to do so.

The prison ombudsman has recorded that federal prisoners die at a much younger age than the Canadian population. The average age of prisoners dying a natural death in custody was sixty-two. And for those who have been released from custody, the average life expectancy is four years shorter than for other Canadians for men (73.4 years of age compared to 77.6) and ten years shorter for women (72.3 compared to 82.9).

OTHER ISSUES

Among the issues that can cause prisoners to strike or even riot is the quality of the food. Good food brings tension down. It makes prisoners feel as if they are people, too. Its nutritional value and the adequacy of portions go a long way to helping maintain order in the prison and to maintaining the health and well-being of the prisoners. Despite this obvious fact, governments continually try to scrimp on the money they spend on food for prisoners. In Ontario, for example, provincial prisons are allotted $9.17 per day for three meals. It is hard to see how anyone could produce an adequate diet on such a budget. In Saskatchewan, poor meals were probably the reason for a recent riot at Prince Albert Penitentiary.

Institutional food is uniformly agreed to be below par. Compass (annual sales of $31 billion) is the company that supplies food to both prisons and hospitals in some parts of Canada. It uses the "Steamplicity" method, wherein the meals are made in a production line in Mississauga, Ontario. These are then sent to their destination where they are microwaved and served. This results in food that is almost all frozen and thus watery and soft when served. It is also highly processed.

When Compass took over food services at the Regina Correctional Centre (saving the government $2.4 million per year), prisoners went on a hunger strike. Premier Brad Wall helpfully remarked, "If you don't like the prison food, don't go to prison." Compass then proceeded to raise its prices at the prison canteen. The canteen is where prisoners often go to supplement their diets with something more palatable. The new higher prices in Regina prompted another hunger strike.

In another ill-advised effort to save money, the federal government cut back on funding for prison chaplains and spiritual leaders. In order to save $1.3 million per year, it decreed that there was no more money to hire part-time chaplains. Since all eighty full-time chaplains were Christian (with the exception of one imam), the change meant that there was essentially no service for minorities. Not only was this clearly discriminatory, it was also regressive from a cost-benefit point of view — the services of chaplains contribute to successful rehabilitation. Ten to 20 percent of prisoners reoffend if they have received these services, compared to 40 to 80 percent if they do not.

This review of the conditions in which Canadian prisoners live is by no means exhaustive but serves to convey their desperate situation. The overuse of segregation, the violence and overcrowding and lockdowns, are unheard of in more advanced prison systems. Over-incarceration of those with mental illness and drug problems, and inadequate treatment of both, are inappropriate and dangerous. Discriminatory practices against aboriginal people and refugees are a blot on our human rights record. Poor treatment of those with physical health problems cannot be justified. The cavalier attitude to providing proper physical and spiritual nourishment is discouraging at the least. It is the recalcitrance of the CSC in dealing with these criticisms and in providing more humane conditions that leads many to believe that the system cannot be reformed, that it must be overhauled completely and replaced with something else.

4

THE DUBIOUS EFFICACY OF REFORMING PRISONS: A GLOBAL VIEW

There is considerable doubt about whether the prison system can ever be reformed so as to produce a positive result. Because we are so risk-averse as a society, we tend to incarcerate far more people than necessary. Then we proceed to treat them harshly, apparently without a thought for the far-reaching consequences of such punishment. Recommending reforms, though, implies that the basic model of incarceration is sound — that it is capable, if properly designed, of producing increased public safety with ex-prisoners returning to their homes as healthy, law-abiding citizens.

Although we say the corrections system is designed to rehabilitate as well as incapacitate people, there is precious little evidence that this obligation is being taken seriously, at least now, at least in Canada. And the question continually arises: how can a system with such a serious imbalance of power between prisoners and staff, operating with virtually no scrutiny by the public, be expected to produce anything but dysfunction and misery?

Guards are suffering from PTSD, prisoners are being mistreated and are mistreating each other, and rehabilitation programs that were once admired internationally are less available. It is certain that many prisoners are being released to their communities bitter and angry, and often sick, both physically and mentally.

Among many of those who work in prisons on a regular basis, there is grave skepticism about the effectiveness of imprisonment. They question whether prisons have ever offered a solution to crime. They say that incarcerating individuals amounts to incarcerating the prisoners' communities. They talk about preventing people from committing crimes in the first place, rather than waiting until people cause harm and then warehousing them in inhumane conditions.

Countless preventive programs have been tried with great success over the years, but we appear not to have the will to continue funding them. The prison-industrial complex, after all, whether privatized or not, provides a lot of jobs in infrastructure and operations. Meanwhile, establishing programs that may take a long time to yield measurable results is not an attractive proposition to politicians whose next test at the ballot box will occur before such results can be achieved.

It is important for our elected representatives, though, to recognize that better jobs and more sensible infrastructure would be produced by adopting a different approach from the old-fashioned "lock 'em up" routine. Creating social programs that require high levels of training in multiple locations across the country makes much more sense than building a few huge prisons dotted around the vast Canadian landscape. Such programs would produce better results with long-lasting effects.

Imagine, for example, if Canada had child care for all, mental health experts to help those who are today falling through the cracks, anger management programs, poverty reduction efforts like a guaranteed annual income, full public dental and drug plans, improved health care and long-term care, treatment for those who have suffered child abuse, assistance for those with PTSD and FASD, comprehensive drug abuse programs, and training and education that provided competent employees for well-paid jobs. These could improve our quality of life and everyone's life prospects to the point where prisons would no longer be required except for those who are truly dangerous. Instead, alternative systems would deal humanely with most of those who do harm. We would have a more equal and healthier society, which would be a boon to all and would assist in further reducing the amount of criminality.

There is an ongoing fundamental disagreement between those who feel the prison system can be adequately reformed and those who insist that a wholesale restructuring of social services is central to creating a workable and effective system for those who break the law. Many of the advocates for a fullscale overhaul argue that trying to reform our prisons merely supports the idea of prisons as a viable option. As Patricia Monture said, if the system is "wrong" from the get-go, then no amount of reform will make it right. But is there not also room for the argument that making some positive impact right now on the lives of prisoners is better than making none?

REFORM IT OR SCRAP IT?

Angela Davis became famous in the 1960s for her civil rights activism. She was involved with the Black Panthers, was a Communist, and went to prison for charges of which she was ultimately cleared. Davis became an author and academic who has written about the racism of the prison system — a subject with which we are familiar in Canada.

In *Abolition Democracy*, Davis says prisons are an abstract concept for most people and that we tend to take them for granted. They are the default position for any ills that beset society. Because we have prisons, we don't have to think about the real issues that concern the communities most affected by the prison system — we just deposit their people into prisons and ignore the underlying problems.

If we can make the case that prisons are racist institutions, Davis argues, we may be able ultimately to consider the prospect of their obsolescence. And some of this argument could be applied to the Canadian context as well, since larger numbers of women and minorities — aboriginal, black, and others — are being incarcerated here than ever before.

Davis argues that reform efforts have merely tended to bolster the legitimacy and permanency of the prison system. Instead, she advocates for decarceration as the central strategy, gradually creating a justice system that is no longer aimed at exacting retribution and vengeance. She sees reconciliation and reparation as the ultimate goal, to be pursued by revitalizing education and providing a full range of physical and mental health care. Alternatives to incarceration must also address a full range of social ills including racism, homophobia, male dominance, and class bias.

This approach to the intractable problems surrounding the current prison system is a good place to start. Davis is not alone in her rejection of efforts merely to reform a broken system.

Todd R. Clear is an expert on criminal justice at Rutgers University. He adopts a similar stance in *Imprisoning Communities: How Mass Incarceration Makes Disadvantaged Neighborhoods Worse*. There he argues that incarceration increases the crime rate by destabilizing the neighbourhoods from which the prisoners come — generally speaking, poor communities. This is a self-perpetuating cycle: incarceration produces the very problems that it is designed to correct. Mark MacGuigan, Louise Arbour, and many others have made this argument in Canada. Clear says reforms will not reduce prisoner numbers because rehabilitation programs, while humane and practical, are only marginally effective at reducing incarceration rates.

Alternatives to incarceration also often fail because those who propose such changes have to guarantee that they will be tough and uncompromising. Otherwise, politicians will not agree to fund them. They also have to guarantee that the public will never be put at risk — an impossible expectation. Proponents of change thus end up designing programs that are so tough that they lead to breaches and violations by ex-prisoners. This in turn leads inevitably back to the default position — more prison.

To avoid these pitfalls, and to provide a system that will succeed in reducing the level of incarceration, Clear calls for "community justice." This would require making community well-being the centre of efforts to deal with crime, much like the restorative justice (RJ) process to be discussed in detail in the next chapter.

Michelle Alexander, in her book *The New Jim Crow: Mass Incarceration in the Age of Colorblindness*, argues that prisons are the new form of slavery and that racism accounts for the large number of African-Americans in U.S. prisons. Likewise, United States Supreme Court Justice Sonia Sotomayor, the first Hispanic judge on that court, has concluded that the criminal justice system is driven by arrogance and machismo and distorted by bad faith and racism.

In Canada, Irvin Waller, a criminologist at the University of Ottawa, is the author of *Less Law, More Order: The Truth About Reducing Crime*. He too asserts that incarceration does not reduce recidivism, and that, to prevent crime, it is better to deal with the reasons why people offend than to try to correct them after the fact. In line with this approach, Waller was instrumental in creating the International Centre for the Prevention of Crime in the 1990s.

In addition to programs that would help prevent crime, Waller says there are things we should be doing to prevent reoffending upon release from prison. To this end, he recommends restorative justice. He says research has shown that this process reduces the likelihood that a wrongdoer will reoffend. Victims also feel much less like retaliating against the person who harmed them, and in many cases are better able to survive the consequences of the offence and get on with their lives.

Critical Resistance is a collective based in the United States that goes much further than recommending preventive programs or other changes to the prison system. It throws down the gauntlet, issuing an indictment of patriarchy, colonization, gender violence, racism, the white supremacist movement, and criminalization of annoying behaviour. It notes that "reform" of the prison system has often merely led to the system's expansion.

Critical Resistance calls for the complete dismantling of the prison-industrial complex. This apparently radical approach stems from a commitment to imagine something better. It recommends learning how to fight for this by forming coalitions of like-minded people who decry both mass incarceration and punishment as the sole objective.

James Kilgore, in *Understanding Mass Incarceration: An Introduction to the Key Civil Rights Struggle of Our Time*, recommends that we pursue policy changes, and agrees that we should link these to other campaigns. For example, advocates for poverty- and inequality-reduction could work together with prison-abolition advocates. Such coalitions could include prisoners, ex-prisoners, and law enforcement personnel who are sympathetic to the cause.

In his forthcoming book, *Locking Up Our Own: Crime and Punishment in Black America*, James Forman Jr. argues that reforms in the U.S. system will come incrementally and at the local level. He says that the input of ex-prisoners is essential, as they are the true experts on the prison system. Those closest to the problem are closest to the solution. Given that nearly one-third of all people in the United States have been arrested by age twenty-three, their voices could be a powerful influence in reforming the system.

Forman also reiterates what we know about victims. He says that if victims are told there are only two alternatives available for offenders — prison or nothing — they will choose prison. But if you tell them that drug treatment, mental health treatment, and/or education are available, they will overwhelmingly choose one of these.

In Canada, *Radical Criminology* (a self-described "insurgent journal") argues for moving "through and beyond" reformist demands. It argues that the reform efforts of academics do not go far enough. Instead, people in the streets and in their neighbourhoods are producing new ideas about replacing law enforcement as we understand it and ultimately abolishing the prison system.

In describing the Downtown East Side of Vancouver (notoriously the most poverty-stricken urban area in Canada), the authors of *Radical Criminology* talk about the relentless targeting and harassment of the poor. Police continually issue tickets for everything from jaywalking to "leaving the curb unsafely," spitting in the street, and transporting goods for sale in a shopping cart. The default sanction for tickets is jail, so people who can't pay are taken into custody. And as one writer notes, jail is very bad for your health. Police also use the tickets to run names for warrants, thus generating a perpetually criminalized population.

There are other radical thinkers who feel the current system is not fixable and would prefer to start over with a better social safety net and the abolition, not just of prisons, but also of "penality" — that is, all notions of punishment and retribution. Many of these proponents are faith communities. It is interesting to note that one of the main such faith groups is the same one that centuries ago designed penitentiaries in the hope of reforming lawbreakers. Today, the Quakers argue strongly against what the prison system has become and are at the forefront of a movement to replace an indefensible system with something that reflects who we are as a civilized people.

CANADA'S EFFORTS TO REFORM

Canada's new federal Liberal government is making some effort to reverse the direction of the previous regime. It is, for example, changing some of the more egregious legislation passed by the Conservative government, but the process is proving to be piecemeal. The changes threaten to do no more than return us to the status quo ante, which is not acceptable. The government should instead begin to decarcerate and to improve conditions immediately. It could start by compelling the CSC to implement the repeated recommendations of the prison ombudsman.

There is little evidence so far that the new government has a vision of corrections that includes wholesale overhaul, or even a reconsideration of the punishment model. Perhaps it is too much to expect this kind of revolutionary thinking from policy-makers, even though crime is declining and they have an opportunity to create something more effective, less expensive, and more humane. As Clear noted, policy-makers rely for their jobs upon their ability to promote changes that the public will approve. Vote-seeking slogans like "tough on crime" or "the war on drugs" are popular, but they are misleading and counterproductive. Radical change to dismantle the tough-on-crime agenda and eventually the punishment model will not come from the top down; it is more likely to come from the ground up, and this will require a concerted effort at public education — not something that is currently on the agenda in Canada.

Prime Minister Trudeau, upon being elected with a majority government in 2015, sent mandate letters to his new minister of justice and attorney general, Jody Wilson-Raybould, and Public Safety Minister, Ralph Goodale, setting out his expectations of their ministries. Justice is mandated to adhere to the *Charter*, to review all changes made by the Conservatives, to legalize marijuana, and to reduce the number of handguns and assault weapons on the street.

Significantly, the prime minister asked Wilson-Raybould to increase the use of restorative justice and other alternative processes to reduce the rate of incarceration of aboriginal people. He also told her to implement the Ashley Smith report recommendations regarding restricting segregation and helping the mentally ill in custody, and to provide sentencing alternatives and reforms to the bail system. The 2017 budget included $57.8 million for mental health treatment for federal prisoners. This is a start when it comes to helping the mentally ill, but it is critical that these funds not serve to further entrench the prison system as the default destination for these prisoners.

Ralph Goodale has been charged with a similar list, but unfortunately there is no direct reference in it to the correctional system, of which he has oversight. This is a bad sign if we expect the new government to deal with deficiencies in the prisons. It remains to be seen whether reversing the tough-on-crime legislation of the previous government will ultimately improve the operations of the CSC, or whether it will merely prevent further deterioration. Evidence of the recent significant curtailment of the use of segregation is promising, but new draft rules recently released by the CSC reflect the old attitude that nothing fundamental needs to change.

Another starting point for the government would be a close examination of the statistics on crime in Canada. While crime has been declining for years, more people are being imprisoned in Canada, mostly for trivial matters and for non-violent, victimless crimes. In 2008, as mentioned earlier, 25 percent of charges were for "administrative" crimes. Another 7 percent or so of crimes in that year were drug possession or trafficking charges with no element of violence. Twenty-three percent were property offences — again with no suggestion of violence. In fact, only about 12 percent of reported offences in Canada are considered violent.

It bears repeating that incarceration largely fails to achieve its stated objectives. It merely provides harsh punishment for all offences, whether low- or high-level, violent or non-violent. It does so with little attention to rehabilitation. It provides a toxic atmosphere that actually encourages further violence and criminality. And it singles out disproportionate numbers of aboriginal people, minorities, the mentally ill, and other disadvantaged Canadians for punishment. This being the case, any reforms to prison conditions should be seen for what they are — a means of alleviating the suffering of prisoners within the system, but not a means of providing a sensible, pragmatic response to crime.

Meanwhile, the large number of non-violent prisoners provides the government with an opportunity to significantly reduce our prison population. The Department of Justice is already reviewing the many mandatory minimum sentences with a view to removing some of them. And it has started an excruciatingly slow process to legalize marijuana. But for the thousands of prisoners currently serving time for trivial and non-violent behaviour, there appears to be no plan. Unlike in the United States, there has been no suggestion of amnesty or reduction of sentences for any of these prisoners.

One of the reasons for the inertia in reform of the prison system is that there are a great many actors whose interests are served by maintaining the status quo. Canada has been building superjails, which greatly benefit the companies hired to construct them. The new Edmonton Remand Centre cost over half a billion dollars and can house 2,800 prisoners. The South Toronto Detention Centre cost more than a billion dollars and can deal with 1,650 prisoners.

In Canada, we have made only one foray into the world of privatized prisons and it failed spectacularly. Central North Correctional Centre in Penetanguishene was built by the Conservative Ontario government to be run by private enterprise. A few short years later, in 2006, the Liberal government had to take it over. Analyses showed that public prisons are superior in providing better security, and better health and recidivism rates.

The policing and court systems in Canada have also been described as huge machines that cost a lot of money and generate a lot of jobs. For example, Vancouver's policing budget was 20 percent of the city's entire budget in 2012. And budgets for the courts are in the billions of dollars. These institutions create jobs, but they do so by supporting a system that ultimately dehumanizes many individuals — prisoners, prison staff, and police. Even more expensive is the warehousing of prisoners themselves. As has already been mentioned, every federal prisoner costs more than $100,000 per year, while provincial prisoners cost somewhat less. This is unsustainable as an economic model. At least as much economic activity would be created by establishing social programs that would alleviate our reliance upon the traditional justice system.

As much as the federal government and the CSC are responsible for deficiencies in a flawed federal system, serious problems exist also at the provincial and local levels. Provinces are responsible for many more prisoners than is the federal government. Currently, there are about forty thousand people in Canadian prisons, only fifteen thousand or so of them in the federal system. And the provincial and territorial systems are rife with problems.

For example, the Ottawa-Carleton Detention Centre (OCDC) has recently been making the news. Media have reported on triple-bunking, as well as prisoners being housed in the showers. At the time of the reports, two prisoners had died at the jail, one of them by suicide. In 2012, a prisoner had given birth there on her jail cell floor. It was a breech birth, and the baby did not survive to its second birthday.

A task force was duly convened to recommend long-term improvements to OCDC and it made a number of detailed, pragmatic, and sensible suggestions. It recommended moving longer-term prisoners to other facilities, exploring the funding of bail beds outside the facility, permitting police to release accused people where appropriate rather than hold them for bail, providing more diversionary programs (drug and mental health treatment), moving health care responsibilities from corrections to the health ministry, conducting a review of health care services, and providing better mental health training for correctional officers. These are achievable recommendations, but the rollout of reforms has not been impressive.

The responsible cabinet minister at the time visited the Ottawa facility and immediately pronounced it to be clean and well-functioning. This was contrary to the task force's observations, which described the jail as messy and dirty. Some minor improvements had been made since the task force reported. A number of new staff had been hired. Prisoners had been given shower sandals, an information booklet had been made available to prisoners, and there was a new coat of paint in the admitting and discharge area. None of the major changes had been tackled, however.

More recently, Ottawa's prison has again been in the news. Just days after the ministry had touted the improvements it had made to health care at OCDC, there was another incident. In January 2017, a pregnant woman was in custody because she failed to turn up at the prison to serve an intermittent sentence. She had also stolen a bottle of vodka from the LCBO and just over $200 worth of goods from a Walmart. Note that these are all non-violent, victimless offences. The woman was in custody for seventeen days before she miscarried her fetus, and she was suffering and bleeding throughout that time. Despite the best efforts of her lawyer to have her taken to a hospital, this was not done. Nobody knows what happened to the fetus, although her lawyer thinks it may have been flushed down a toilet.

This also happened in the twenty-first century in Canada, and it happened despite the excellent recommendations of a task force designed to prevent such inhumane treatment. The provincial ministry, though, appears to feel no urgency or responsibility about implementing necessary reforms. In a similar vein, reports in early 2017 show there were three suicides in ten months at OCDC. It normally takes three to seven years to obtain an inquest into a death in custody, and the authorities appear not to be moving urgently in these cases.

Nova Institution for Women in Nova Scotia is also acquiring a poor reputation for its treatment of prisoners. In 2015, two women died in that prison, one because she received improper medical treatment. The other, who was known to have a mental illness, suicided. Nova does try to help its pregnant prisoners, allowing an organization called Women's Wellness Within to provide doula birthing services. But clearly there is a serious problem at Nova.

Kim Pate has thirty-five years of experience in prisons. She notes that very few of these incarcerated women pose any risk to public safety at all. The prisons are simply poorhouses, where women are put because there is nowhere else for them to be. The system is hierarchical and paramilitary, and the prisons attempt to control all information. When Pate first visited the Prison for Women in Kingston (P4W) after the 1994 incident that resulted in the Arbour Report, she remarked to the warden that she had seen women in shackles. The warden directly contradicted her, saying that "no woman is in shackles."

There are some good-news stories, too. It's not as though Canadians don't know how to run a prison with some measure of decency and humanity. In Mission, British Columbia, there is place called Emma's Acres where victims work together with people who have been convicted of breaking the law. The farm is run by an ex-prisoner who served twenty years for murder. He says he eventually met the daughter of the person he had killed, and this allowed him to fully understand what he had done. Now he is making up for it as best he can.

One volunteer at the farm is the father of a victim of Clifford Olson. It is astonishing that the father of one of these children would find it within himself to work with prisoners. But he says that helping these men helps him to deal with the loss. He says that he has changed his attitude toward men who have made a mistake and are trying to make up for it. He wants to help. What an astonishing commentary this is on the ability of human beings to feel compassion in the face of the worst harm imaginable.

Emma's Acres is one project that works toward re-habilitation and reconciliation — all so necessary for people to deal with their pain, whatever shape it takes. Canada could be doing much more. In the face of inertia by governments, Canadian communities are taking up the challenge and creating programs designed to change the conditions that lead to imprisonment. Countless grassroots programs are directed at preventing crime and assisting ex-prisoners in order to reduce recidivism and improve reintegration with the community. These efforts target the well-known risk factors for crime: previous abuse, drug dependency, poverty, unemployment, mental illness, and so on. They provide essential services that successfully reduce rates of antisocial behaviour in hopes of reducing the rate of incarceration. Positive though these efforts are, they are not always coordinated and are often run on a shoe-string. They largely succeed in their objectives but they are not designed to call into question the fundamental efficacy of wholesale incarceration.

Prisoners themselves are finding ways to effect change for the better. I am reminded of one of the more heartening things I have seen in a prison. The Special Olympics (an athletic competition for people with intellectual disabilities) were being held behind the wall at Collins Bay Institution in Kingston. It is a medium-security prison, and a lot of the men there had reputations for violence. But they organized and operated the entire day of athletic events and it was a huge success.

They assigned each prisoner to be a "Big Brother" to one of the contestants. It was quite something to see — burly, tattooed gang members and enforcers doing their jailhouse strut hand-in-hand with little children with Down Syndrome or other disabilities. They cheered those kids on to the finish line and hugged them at the end and everybody had a great day.

Who knows how much rehabilitation was achieved on that simple occasion, where prisoners were trusted and given responsibility? They took on a challenge and showed their ability to organize and also to empathize with their young charges. I am told that the Special Olympics were still being held at Collins Bay as recently as a few years ago. I hope so. These are occasions that can help prisoners realize they have some useful skills and can make a contribution. For those of us on the outside, it helps us recognize their humanity and see that there is no "us versus them." We are all in this together.

THE UNITED STATES' EFFORTS TO REFORM

Canada has been among the last Western countries to start reforming its prison system in a more progressive way. While we were struggling under the tough-on-crime mandate of the Conservative government from 2006 to 2015, the United States, for example, was already moving to decarcerate. True, this was often less for altruistic reasons than because huge numbers of prisoners (2.2 million at last count) were placing heavy strains on budgets.

Nonetheless, during the Obama administration, there was an unlikely alliance of Republicans and Democrats in an organization called Right on Crime. Hard-right politicians like Newt Gingrich began to work with the American Civil Liberties Union and others in an effort to achieve criminal justice reform, beginning with a reduction in the prison population.

Converts like Republican Pat Nolan also put their weight behind the reform effort. Nolan was a hard-line law-and-order advocate until he went to prison himself in the 1990s. His change of heart illustrates the maxim: "If a conservative is a liberal who has been mugged, a liberal is a conservative who has served time." Unlike some, Nolan maintains that reform should not be about saving money; instead, it should be about preserving human dignity. He says that incarcerating non-violent people is counterproductive and is something that only a rich and vindictive people would do.

Conservatives and liberals had, by 2015, found common ground on the central objective of reforming the policing and prison systems. They came up with a number of ideas and programs that are pragmatic and can be implemented easily.

These included reducing the number of mandatory minimums, eliminating cash bail, using probation and other alternatives to prison for low-level crime, raising the age for juveniles, limiting segregation, no longer allowing police to confiscate assets, using prison less often as punishment for technical infractions of probation and parole, providing education and job training in prison, allowing prisoners time off for rehabilitation, and reducing obstacles caused by criminal records.

Unfortunately, the legislation that would have accomplished much of this stalled in a gridlocked Congress, and — now that the Trump administration has taken over — it is unlikely to be revived. President Trump has appointed Jeff Sessions as his attorney general — the same Jeff Sessions who was instrumental in blocking the bipartisan 2015 Sentencing Reform bill and who is a hard-line drug warrior. He has already announced a new crackdown on drug use, saying marijuana is as dangerous as heroin. He once supported legislation that would have made a second marijuana trafficking conviction a capital crime; that is, it would have attracted the death penalty. Upon his appointment, he immediately instructed his federal prosecutors to pursue the most serious charges possible against the vast majority of suspects, which is a direct reversal of Obama's policies. Criminal justice advocates say this is a return to MMSs (mandatory minimum sentences) and a modern "Stone Age" policy. Former attorney general Eric Holder calls it "dumb on crime," rather than "tough on crime."

In 2015, a group of American police chiefs, prosecutors, and sheriffs also came together to push for alternatives to arrests, reducing the number of crimes on the books, and ending mandatory minimums. Significantly, they said the country needs less incarceration, not more, to keep citizens safe. Law enforcement officers asked Trump to abandon his crackdown on crime, but the president ignored them and signed a tough-on-crime executive order anyway.

The Brennan Center for Justice recently surveyed 1.5 million prisoners in the United States and concluded that a quarter of them could have been spared incarceration without jeopardizing public safety. It said that a further 14 percent had already served enough time and could safely be released. The Major Cities Chiefs Association and the National District Attorneys Association have both argued for scaling back mass incarceration, as well.

Large-scale reform is still not on the horizon, but in the dying days of his presidency, President Obama did issue clemency orders to about one thousand prisoners. He also used executive orders to reduce the use of segregation, scale back federal drug prosecutions, and eliminate prison privatization. These orders are now being systematically reversed by the new president. All of these measures only apply to the federal system, which represents a small fraction of those incarcerated in the United States, but there has been more action on the prison reform front at the state level, where many states are rethinking their approach to criminal justice. Texas — arguably the most conservative state in the union — began financing drug treatment and mental health services, as well as improving post-release supervision, long before Right on Crime came along. Drug-treatment programs enabled the state to close one prison in 2011 and two more in 2013. The rate of growth of the state's prison population has slowed impressively.

Between 2007 and 2015, Texas had cut its incarceration rates from 678 per 100,000 to 588 — still vastly more than any other country in the world (Canada's rate is in the range of 110), but an impressive improvement nonetheless. Nine out of fourteen young-offender units are now closed. There are specialist courts for substance abuse, domestic violence, juveniles, women, and veterans. During the same period, contrary to tough-on-crime orthodoxy, crime declined by 27 percent and recidivism also dropped.

Reformers insist that any savings from their reforms be placed back into the social system to help ex-prisoners succeed on the outside. Failing to do so causes its own problems. California is a good example. Ordered by the Supreme Court to downsize its prison populations, the state did succeed in reducing its numbers by 25 percent in five years. But because funding was not put into services for ex-prisoners and their communities, California experienced a downloading to local jails, which then increased in number. There was also an increase in homelessness and in the number of mentally ill people who were not receiving treatment.

There are many other examples of how the states are trying to reduce their incarceration rates. Mississippi has avoided further increases in its prison population by making non-violent prisoners eligible for parole after 25 percent of their sentences rather than the previous standard of 85 percent. The state has reduced its prison population by 15 percent.

In South Carolina, non-violent drug users and dealers are no longer automatically sent to prison, but can be considered for probation. Post-release and parole supervision have also been improved so that fewer ex-prisoners end up back in prison for breaching parole. North Carolina was expected to save about $250 million over five years in prison building and operating costs.

Florida created a Criminal Mental Health Project that provides training for police in dealing with people suffering from mental health problems. As a result, Miami police arrested just nine out of more than ten thousand people in response to mental health calls in 2013, where previously most of these cases would have led to arrests. Let me repeat that: the number went from a potential of several thousand arrests down to nine.

New York State has reduced its prison population by twenty thousand since 1999 and has closed five prisons in the last five years. It has greatly reduced the number of arrests for things like begging for a Metrocard or sleeping in the subway.

By 2016, the number of states trying to reduce incarceration rates had increased significantly. Reforms included giving judges more power to release accused people on cashless bail (New Jersey), creating twenty-four-hour crisis centres to keep mentally ill people from being locked up (Idaho), establishing courts for military veterans accused of crimes (Georgia and Louisiana), and funding programs to reunify children with parents who were incarcerated (Hawaii).

South Dakota has a new program for drunk drivers and for domestic assault perpetrators whose offences involve alcohol. These people must go to a police station twice a day and blow into the breathalyzer. If they fail to attend or if they fail the breathalyzer test, they serve two days in jail. According to a Rand Institute analysis, the breach rate is less than 1 percent.

Despite the continued war on drugs, Utah has taken the unprecedented step of reducing possession of heroin or cocaine from a felony to a misdemeanour, allowing judges to impose shorter sentences or no prison term at all. Several states have now legalized marijuana for both medical and recreational use, and others have decriminalized simple possession of the drug. An Ohio judge who is currently considering running for governor is arguing for legalization of marijuana and the release of all non-violent marijuana offenders from prison.

Hawaii has a program called HOPE (Hawaii's Opportunity Probation with Enforcement). It has cut drug offences significantly by changing its approach to parole or probation violations by those convicted of drug crimes. Instead of revoking and reincarcerating ex-prisoners, the program applies swift and moderated sanctions.

In California, when sentences for low-level drug and property offences were lowered in 2014, prison populations actually dropped, to the surprise of many who said they were bound to spike. It became clear that public safety did not depend on harsh sentencing.

Also in California, a controversial program called the Office of Neighborhood Safety (ONS) was initiated in 2007 in Richmond in a desperate attempt to stem pervasive violence. This program was mainly designed for ex-prisoners in an effort to curb recidivism. It is ground-breaking, counterintuitive, and controversial, and it represents a real work of the imagination. It has also enjoyed considerable success.

The ONS is run mainly by ex-convicts. It targets young men who are most likely to kill or be killed in an area where gang murders proliferate. The ONS program provides incentives to men with firearms records to stop the violence. First, it gives the men social services referrals and life-skills training to find work and get an education. Later, and more controversially, it adds a monthly cash payment and supervised trips outside the city.

The result? In 2007, Richmond was the ninth most dangerous city in the United States with forty-seven murders in a population of 106,000. By 2014, under the ONS program, the murder rate had dropped to fifteen per 100,000, the lowest rate in thirty-three years. The murder rate across the country had dropped during the same time period, but Richmond was exceptional.

The director of ONS said that at the time it was created local people did not trust law enforcement, and community services were poor. He decided that the only way to combat the violence was to do so without the involvement of police. When he learned that most of the violence was being perpetrated by just a handful of people, he targeted those individuals and invited them to a meeting where they were treated with respect and given lunch at the city manager's office. If they agreed to participate in the new, voluntary Operation Peacemaker Fellowship, the $1,000 they would receive at the end of the meeting would be just the beginning of regular payments. Sixty-eight participants took part in the program and sixty-four of them are still alive.

My first inclination was to question the wisdom of paying people to stop shooting each other. But the evidence is that the payments fall far short of the budget that would otherwise be required to pay for police overtime, criminal prosecution, and helicopter medivac rides for victims. And, more to the point, the murder rate fell precipitously. That is a truly astonishing track record.

The ONS went even further. It offered trips outside Richmond. The participants went to New York, Washington, and even overseas, and stayed in good hotels with good meals and access to professional athletes and politicians. But there was a catch. Each participant had to travel with a member of a rival gang. In the end, it didn't take long for these sworn enemies to realize that they had a lot in common and that they could get along together. In other words, the program broke down the "us-versus-them" attitude, promoting public safety along the way.

Contributing to the success of the Richmond experiment was a new city council that hired a progressive police chief. He was more interested in what works to prevent crime than in an ideological, moralistic approach to punishing those who break the law. This refreshing attitude could be emulated elsewhere. The new chief made policing more community-oriented and actually gave people gift cards in return for their guns.

Winning the police over to the ONS program, though, was understandably a challenge. One officer admitted that the ONS had finally won his trust because they were not a bunch of "bunny huggers" trying to tell him these men were not dangerous. They *were* dangerous. Also, the officer understood that, while these men did not "deserve" the money they were being given, life was more complicated than that. He understood that, by definition, "mercy" is extended to those who may not appear to merit it.

This, too, is an important lesson for police and others involved in the criminal justice system. The issues are not black and white: they are complex, and require complex solutions. We can't just say "Lock 'em up up and throw away the key." If we do, we perpetuate an untenable situation and jeopardize public safety. Thus, complicated and thoughtful solutions like the ONS need to be considered for every part of the system.

There are myriad other stories of how individual jurisdictions have sought to reduce their rates of incarceration and deal with relatively petty matters in a less draconian way. Pushed by a federal court ruling, a small city in Montana agreed in 2016 to pay $4.7 million to compensate people who had been incarcerated for failing to pay fines and fees relating to petty violations. The city from then on was required to determine whether or not a person was *able* to pay the fine before making an order that could result in a prison sentence. The Montana settlement put an end to using the courts as a means of generating revenue rather than dispensing justice — some cities had been relying upon fines for more than 40 percent of their general revenues.

In the category of not-at-all-petty matters, in 2016 Mississippi required the local government of one of its counties to reduce its incarceration rate in the wake of horrific stories of prison violence, human rights violations, and a failure to release prisoners on their release dates. A criminal justice coordinating committee was formed comprising judges, sheriffs, mental health professionals, and local residents. They were charged with creating alternatives to incarceration and with helping to ease the transition out of prison through assistance with housing, job training, and mental health treatment.

Such examples of innovative and successful alternatives to incarceration are encouraging, but there are other, less hopeful, trends. One of these in the United States reflects its current neoliberal, market-driven philosophy — the trend to privatize prisons and outsource prison services. It is estimated that more than half of all state and local prisons and jails have outsourced health care services — resulting in costs running to about $3 billion per year. This is despite the fact that it costs so much more to go private. Budgets increased 24 percent from 2010 to 2014 in federal prisons. Of the sixty-nine prisons surveyed, all of them paid much more for medical services than the Medicare rates — as much as 385 percent more.

One private company making huge profits from the prison system is CoreCivic (formerly the Corrections Corporation of America or CCA). Canadians were alarmed to hear in 2012 that the Conservative government was contemplating offering contracts to CCA to provide certain services. This was at the same time that CCA and other companies were lobbying for new contracts in the wake of a push to reduce incarceration and close prisons in the United States.

CCA wrote to American states offering to buy up their prisons and run them in return for a guarantee that the prisons would be kept at 90 percent occupancy. The implications of this are shocking — states would be expected to provide a steady supply of prisoners in exchange for divesting themselves of the responsibility of operating a prison system.

One of the largest private companies that runs prisons in the United States is Management and Training Corp. In 2016, one of its prisons, Walnut Grove in Mississippi, was closed because of human rights violations, appalling brutality, lawlessness, and sexual misconduct. The rape of young prisoners by others was common. Guards were having sex with prisoners, while denying medical care to some and smuggling weapons and drugs into the institution. Guards were gang members. Frequent gladiator-style fights were organized between prisoners and bet on by guards. One month after Walnut Grove was closed, the Justice Department announced that it was phasing out its use of private prisons for federal prisoners because they were less effective and more dangerous than those run by the government. Unfortunately, one of President Trump's first executive orders reversed this decision, thus allowing privatization to continue.

Although the reforms described above are piecemeal and rely largely upon individual states to take action, it is clear that there is an appetite for changing the U.S. approach to criminal justice. So far, there is no plan to overhaul the whole system from policing to courts to prisons, but the reforms at least lessen the suffering and misery of those already in prison, and ensure that there will be fewer prisoners in the future.

MODELS FROM FARTHER AFIELD

Prison reform outside of Canada and the United States is rather a mixed bag. In Britain, then prime minister David Cameron in 2015 placed prison reform at the heart of a new "compassionate conservatism." Half of Britain's prisoners reoffend upon release, so it was past time to adopt a new and more evidence-based approach. But that was 2015, and today the country is led by Theresa May, a hard-liner on crime. Her justice secretary, Liz Truss, has suggested that prisons should be tough, unpleasant, and uncomfortable.

It is safe to say that this is already true of Britain's prisons. Violence levels are through the roof. In the first six months of 2015, 105 prisoners killed themselves, compared with 59 in 2010. Self-harm incidents have increased, and serious assaults against other prisoners and guards have gone up exponentially.

Eight people had been murdered in prison by June in 2015, compared to none in 2012.

Significantly, the British prison service was required to cut its budget by a quarter between 2010 and 2015. In 2015, the riot squad was called out more than 340 times, compared with 118 calls in 2010. At the same time, the number of front-line officers was down by a quarter. So many officers are quitting that new hires can barely keep up. Nearly a fifth of all prisoners spend less than two hours a day outside their cells, and some get only thirty minutes. England and Wales are thus ripe for reform, but the new regime's approach is not encouraging.

More encouraging is the transformation of prison systems in such disparate nations as Latvia, Nicaragua, Rwanda, Brazil, and Australia. Scandinavian countries still set the standard for humane treatment and successful results, but many other jurisdictions are working hard to improve systems that over-incarcerate and hold people in inhumane conditions.

Latvia was for decades in the orbit of the former Soviet Union. It had a high incarceration rate of 337 per 100,000 of population when it joined the European Union in 2004. The EU average was 122 per 100,000. By 2015, Latvia had trimmed its rate to around 200.

Latvians said that they had always thought there was no alternative to prison. This accords with the default position that prisons have assumed in Canada. But Latvia began to employ alternatives to prison, such as more community service orders (CSOs) and more electronic monitoring. These solutions are not an automatic fix for high incarceration rates, though, as in many jurisdictions they merely lead to net-widening. That is, the CSOs and electronic monitoring become additional to rather than instead of prison sentences, and are applied freely for minor infractions. Such sentences become more about control than about rehabilitation.

Latvia was an exception to the net-widening phenomenon, however. This is partly because its budget dictated a need to reduce incarceration rates. The country could not afford the high numbers, so it cut sentences for non-violent offences and decriminalized some others.

In 2012, Nicaragua, one of the poorest countries in Latin America, boasted an incarceration rate of only 120 per 100,000 people — a low rate compared with nearby El Salvador, which had a rate of 390. The country was also less violent than Panama and was nearing the low rate established by Costa Rica. As well as low incarceration rates, Nicaragua also has relatively low rates of violent crime. Neighbouring Honduras had 82 murders per 100,000 people in 2010; Nicaragua had just 13.

These low rates are not a result of Nicaragua having limitless funding for crime control. It can afford only 18 police for every 10,000 people, and these police are the worst paid in the region. But the woman who leads the police force (a former nun and guerrilla fighter) says that Nicaraguans did not want to pursue the "*mano dura*" (iron fist) of their neighbours. They saw enough of that during the 1979 revolt against dictator Anastasio Somoza.

Instead, the country makes use of an army of one hundred thousand volunteers, who include law and psychology students; ten thousand former gang members, who mentor youth via baseball in the barrios; and four thousand domestic violence victims, who persuade women to speak out. Confidence in the police is the highest in Latin America after Chile.

Baz Dreisinger, author of *Incarceration Nations: A Journey to Justice in Prisons Around the World*, undertook to visit countries around the world to see their prisons. She started in Rwanda, where in 1994 eight hundred thousand people were murdered in one hundred days. Those who had murdered and maimed tens of thousands were incarcerated in shocking conditions. This changed, though, when a process based upon traditional African justice was instituted and thousands of them were released.

The treatment of those who remained in prison, Dreisinger found, was surprisingly different from that afforded in American prisons. Guards carried no guns. There was almost no violence. Correctional officers did not even have to enter the prison, because order was maintained by a prisoner-run government. And most of the leaders were *genocidaires* — those who had committed genocide in 1994. Prisoners were allowed to go outside the prison to work and they all had access to the internet. Guards and prisoners played football together. One guard told Dreisinger that there was really no difference between "them and us."

This last comment brought to mind a conversation I had with a former prison guard in Canada who now runs a preventive program for youth. We had been sharing our stories about prison life when he said to me, "Do you know the difference between a guard and a prisoner?" He then answered his own question by holding up his hand with his thumb and index finger about a millimetre apart. In other words, no real difference.

Dreisinger found that some countries, like Uganda and Jamaica, provide rehabilitation through writing and music and other arts. In Brazil, prisoners can reduce their sentences by reading books and writing summaries of them. They can earn up to forty-eight days per year off their sentences this way — a real incentive to participate.

Dreisinger also visited prisons in Australia, where she found even the worst of the privatized prisons to be an improvement over prisons in the United States. The best of them allowed prisoners to move about freely. There were no uniforms. It was impossible to tell who was a prisoner and who was staff. The prisoners ran the prison and were also allowed to work off-site. There was a heavy emphasis on rehabilitation.

SCANDINAVIA

The nations with the highest standards in their prisons and the lowest incarceration rates are in Scandinavia. Hewing to their fundamental belief in generous social services and the importance of caring for one another, these Nordic nations also have some of the best success rates among released prisoners. Nils Christie of Norway says that prison is the "intended delivery of pain." But Scandinavians recognize that the pain or punishment consists in the loss of freedom only, and not also in a disregard of basic needs or rights — certainly not also in the harsh conditions that have characterized Canadian prisons.

Nordic prisons are smaller than those in Canada and the United States. The largest of them houses only 350 prisoners, but more common are prisons holding only a hundred or so. Having multiple small prisons spread around the country ensures that prisoners remain closer to their families, which encourages the maintaining of all-important family bonds and community connections. Canada's experiment with local prisons for women has not succeeded on the same scale, but the model is still one to be emulated if we can adjust our system to fully adopt Norway's best practices.

Rehabilitative programs are central to the operation of Norwegian prisons, and because conditions in the prisons are relatively agreeable, these programs have a chance at success. All levels of education are offered as a right. The model for occupational programs is embedded in the community, so that there is a likelihood of prisoners finding employment upon release. All health care is regarded as a right, so mental health and substance-abuse programs are made available to all who need them.

One of the more startling differences between Nordic prisons and our own is the care taken to choose and train candidates for the job of prison guard. In Canada, candidates must have secondary education (Grade 12) and a course in First Aid and CPR. Training consists of four weeks of online learning, four weeks of assignments, and ten to eleven weeks of training, mainly with use-of-force equipment. In Nordic countries, candidates must also have secondary education, but the training period is significantly longer, ranging from a total of twenty weeks in Sweden to three years in Norway and Finland.

In Norway, the training is at the level of university or college education. Guards are taught a long list of subjects: law, environment, safety, ethics, human rights, professionalism, values, cultural understanding, mental health, effects of isolation, and so on. Guards vary by education, gender, and age and theirs is a sought-after job. A guard's attitude is thought to directly influence success. Guards are expected to show respect for prisoners, and to act in ways that generate hope rather than despair. They are taught that prisoners must be kept busy, to control aggression levels.

The philosophy of the correctional service is that prisoners will reoffend if they have to serve very long sentences, if the discipline is too strict, if there are "shock" programs (like Scared Straight, a program of American origin where youngsters are taken into high-security prisons and harassed and frightened by the toughest prisoners), or if there are regular sanctions like the withdrawal of coveted privileges such as telephone calls and visits. The more restrictive the surroundings, the harder it is for prisoners to live peacefully and the less safe the prison becomes. Prisoners are also known to do better when there is lots of interaction with qualified personnel.

Physically, Norwegian prisons are more like schools. They have coloured walls, paintings, poetry, friendly guards, and no batons or Kevlar vests, even in maximum security (although the prisoners in these sections are locked up). Violence against guards is extremely rare.

At Bastøy, an "open" or minimum-security prison, the staff and prisoners work together gathering potatoes and doing other work. Four to six prisoners live together in houses, travelling out of the prison to work, coming back on nights and weekends. They are expected to look after the houses, make their own meals, and so on. On weekends there are 4 guards for 115 prisoners with the guards staying in a separate building. Such is the degree of trust afforded the prisoners that one chainsaw-killer served the final part of his sentence at Bastøy, working in the woods — with a chainsaw.

When Baz Dreisinger visited Bastøy, she reported that staff had no fear of the prisoners, played cards with them, and interacted with them normally. Wanting to learn more about the thinking behind this way of operating a prison, Dreisinger spoke with the prison warden. Interestingly, the warden (his title is "governor") had worked in a more traditional, U.S.-style prison for twenty-two years. This experience taught him that that model was a failure. He told her that people operate such prisons only because they are lazy. He did admit to being skeptical when he first came to Bastøy, but now believes almost all prisons should be "open." Constructing an entire prison system designed to deal with dangerous people but catching up thousands of non-violent people as well — as we do in Canada and the United States, in order to avoid all risk — is a mistake.

Halden prison in Norway opened in 2012. A "closed" (maximum-security) prison sitting on seventy-five acres, it nonetheless has no bars on windows and doors. There is a full kitchen and many vocational programs, including a recording studio. Halden houses about the same number of staff as prisoners and is a progressive prison with private visiting rooms. Within the prison there are ample opportunities for rehabilitation, including a restaurant school, a landscaping class, and a print shop.

Prison staff say that short sentences and good accommodations make sense. After all, the prisoners either go back to society angry and aggressive or rehabilitated and capable of fitting back into their communities. Norwegian authorities insist that it is important to treat prisoners like human beings and not like animals. As a result, Norway has one of the lowest recidivism rates in the world at 20 percent, and a relatively low level of crime as well, most of it property crime.

Nils Christie is an expert on prison systems and the author of *Crime Control as Industry: Towards Gulags, Western Style*. He says there must be limits to the number of people we choose to incarcerate. And, make no mistake, we do choose. The number of prisoners is not driven by crime rates but by the tenor of the times, the prevailing politics, and the amount of fear that has been instilled in the populace. The Norwegian system shows that high incarceration rates can be avoided without compromising public safety and provides a decent and humane response to criminal behaviour. It should be emulated.

Doing so is not easy, of course. Christie points out that Scandinavian countries have some natural advantages — they are more homogeneous than some, and this confers an advantage: they are able to institutionalize mercy in ways that are not always available to more complex populations. Dreisinger discusses this relative homogeneity as well, referring to the Norwegian notion of "*janteloven*" it encourages. This is the opposite of American individualism, and represents instead a culture of volunteerism and community participation.

One small aspect of the criminal justice system in Norway serves to illustrate the difference between its prison system (and that of many European countries) and ours. In Canada, when an accused is sentenced he or she is taken immediately into custody and then sent to prison. Because of this, defence counsel tell their clients to bring their toothbrush to court because they might be going straight to prison. There will be no opportunity to arrange their affairs, pack a bag, or say goodbye to anyone.

In Norway, people sentenced to custody first go home. They later receive a letter telling them when and where to appear to serve their sentence. Some even meet with police and discuss when it would be best for them to serve their time. Ninety-five percent of these people turn up at the appointed time. If there are not enough spaces in the system, instead of cramming prisoners into cells made for one person, the Norwegians create a waiting list. This is a recognition that those on the list can be trusted not to reoffend.

Finland could also teach us some lessons about running a criminal justice system. K.J. Lång was director general for many years of the Finnish prison system. He too said that the number of people incarcerated had nothing to do with the crime rate. The high rate of incarceration in Finland decades ago (due to the country's emulation of its neighbour, the Soviet Union) was seen as a problem and nothing to be proud of. The authorities knew they could bring down the numbers without repercussions on the street, and they did.

Tapio Lappi-Seppälä of Finland says there is an inverse relationship between a country's commitment to the welfare of its citizens and its rate of incarceration. Good social policy, he says, is the best criminal justice policy, because it helps to prevent crime and rehabilitate wrongdoers. The more that trust in society declines and fear escalates, the more punitive will be the criminal justice system. He regards the Nordic system as pragmatic and non-moralistic.

Suomenlinna Island prison in Finland is a good example of the Scandinavian model of incarceration. This minimum-security prison, which houses ninety-five prisoners (including murderers) is located right beside a major Finnish tourist attraction, a UNESCO World Heritage site. This, however, appears to present no problems at all. Indeed, the prisoners are allowed to leave the prison every day to go to work on the mainland. The prison system thinks that it is important to allow this since the prisoners are getting ready for release and need to reacclimatize to life outside a prison. Inside the prison, the cells are like dormitories and prisoners may visit family and friends in Helsinki while wearing electronic monitors. Prisoners and staff sit down to their meals together. They wear their own clothes. The officers carry no weapons. Staff are rewarded for interacting and empathizing with prisoners, and not for providing harsh treatment.

Kerava open prison in Finland has rabbits and sheep for the prisoners to care for, as well as a greenhouse. There are no locks and no uniforms. Prisoners are able to shop for groceries in town, take three days' vacation every couple of months, and go on supervised camping and fishing trips. They are paid for their work ($8 per hour compared with $6.90 per day in Canada), and must pay rent to the prison and a subsidy if they go to university. This program is meant to prepare prisoners for reintroduction to a normal life upon release. If a prisoner tries to escape, he will go to a closed facility. Closed (maximum) prisons are still comfortable places, however. They also have humanizing aspects, like pool tables, aquaria, and dart boards. There is never any overcrowding.

Not only are prisoners better looked after in Scandinavian prisons, so, too, are the guards. In Suomenlinna Island, guards are responsible for rehabilitation, and not just for security. Thus guards can do their jobs without suffering the mental damage that may be caused by a regime that simply provides punishment. In the United States, guards have an average life expectancy of only fifty-nine years and PTSD rates are high. Finland tries to avoid this kind of consequence to its staff. Scandinavians want to have nothing to do with systems that commit every crime against their prisoners that those prisoners have themselves committed on the outside. To do so would be to perpetuate the original harm.

Sweden follows much the same template as Finland and Norway. The prison system's director general says his role is not to punish. Any idea of caging and dehumanizing is simply not in the ken of Swedish authorities. As elsewhere in Scandinavia, staff are like social workers, dedicated to preparing prisoners for release by treating them with dignity and respect.

Denmark is the fourth Scandinavian country and it takes a similar approach. Open prisons provide cells with TVs, computers, sound systems, and cell phones. Note that cell phones are particularly forbidden in some Canadian prisons because of concerns about people making drug deals and running other criminal enterprises from inside the prison. Denmark seems to be able to deal with these concerns, thus allowing for a very important connection for prisoners with their family and friends.

Prisoners cook their own meals, wear their own clothes, and see their families privately. There are no walls or gun towers: officials say it is better to have an escape than a hostage-taking. It is recognized that some prisoners will break the rules, but the staff still do not do cavity searches because the dignity of the prisoners is a priority. Sixty thousand leaves from prison are granted every year, and only 3 percent of the prisoners violate the terms of the leave or fail to return. Escapes are rare. There is little violence and the prison staff feel safe. The recidivism rate is half that in the United States.

The Danish system does incarcerate far more ethnic minorities than can be justified by their proportion in the population. And it is agreed that solitary confinement is used too often. However, humane treatment is the fundamental philosophy — not the zero tolerance that can lead to escapes, drug use, recidivism, and violence of all kinds. Prisoners are allowed to make mistakes without forfeiting everything. The most serious consequence is removal to a closed setting.

With all of these examples of humane prisons and low incarceration rates, the question then becomes, what should we be doing differently in Canada? To institute something like the Scandinavian model would be a huge improvement. But should we stop at trying to make prisons fewer and more humane, or should we take on the larger task of providing complete alternatives to prisons? Can processes like restorative justice help us deal with wrongdoing? Can we find ways to separate those who are dangerous while abolishing prison for all other purposes?

5

RESTORATIVE JUSTICE AND OTHER ALTERNATIVES

Restorative justice (RJ) processes offer an alternative to traditional forms of criminal justice in many countries around the world. Canada, England, Australia, Scotland, New Zealand, Norway, the United States, Japan, and several European countries have all adopted forms of RJ to some degree. Restorative justice regards crime as an injury to people and relationships. It recognizes that harm has been done to individuals and not just to the state. Our current approach creates a fiction that sets up the accused against the state. It fixes blame and then applies retribution. It does not give the victim a significant role in the proceedings, but allows a Crown attorney to represent the victim. RJ proposes a different approach.

Restorative justice aims to restore a victim's losses, hold lawbreakers accountable (which they do by accepting responsibility and paying reparations), and build peace in the community. The approach is holistic, concentrating on restitution and reconciliation as well as the restoration of harmony in the community.

In the RJ process, trained facilitators prepare both the victim and the person who harmed him or her for a face-to-face meeting. This happens only if both parties agree to meet voluntarily, and it may occur in the presence and with the participation of the community. The parties discuss the offence and how it has affected them. They then try to arrive at a solution, which may involve paying for damages, doing community service, seeking treatment for underlying problems, and so on. Canada's department of public safety (Public Safety Canada) has put its imprimatur on this process and states that the goal is to encourage healing, repair the harm, and reintegrate the wrongdoer into his or her community.

The objective of RJ, though, is not to completely replace the traditional criminal justice system. In fact, even where RJ has been used in a case, the offender may still be judged as dangerous and may ultimately need to be incarcerated. Having said that, it's important to note that RJ is not used just for minor offences. It can be used with success for very serious crimes, including murder. Most RJ systems are not applied to sex assault or family violence situations because of the particular power dynamic involved in these, and because the safety of the victim must always be paramount. Yet, we will see that the system worked very well for such offences in Hollow Water First Nation in Manitoba.

Some skeptics feel that RJ represents a move toward being "soft on crime." However, wrongdoers who have benefited from RJ say that it is much tougher to go through a process where they face their victims than it is to spend time in prison. Important, too, according to the Canadian Resource Centre for Victims of Crime, is that victims themselves have been the driving force behind the use of RJ. They can choose this method of justice knowing that they will not be pressured into participating, and that facilitators will ensure that they are not.

A meta-analysis of RJ in Canada found that there were measurable positive outcomes. Victims who participated were significantly more satisfied than those who went through traditional courts. There were substantially higher compliance rates with restitution and reparations, and recidivism rates under RJ were much lower than for those going to traditional courts.

A more recent study on the effects of RJ in Australia and England also concluded that these were very positive. Victims were less fearful of a repeat attack from the same person in the case of assault, and they were more pleased with the way their cases were handled. There was a measurable reduction in recidivism. One study from England found that 27 percent fewer crimes were being committed by individuals who had been through the RJ process. And victims who had been through the process experienced fewer symptoms of PTSD.

It is important to note that Canada occupies a special position in the development of restorative justice, along with Australia and New Zealand. All three countries have aboriginal populations that have been marginalized for centuries and mistreated by Eurocentric criminal justice systems. And all three countries now see the efficacy of traditional aboriginal justice systems and are adopting some of their features wholesale, as with the RJ projects noted above. Why? Because they work, and because their proponents are less interested in confrontation, adversarial processes, and punishment.

Many victims harbour no anger or hate, and actually ask judges not to sentence the persons who harmed them to lengthy prison sentences. The ability to do this is not given to everyone, but for those who do, there is a recognition that hate and anger will ruin their lives far beyond the damage caused by the offender. It is one objective of aboriginal justice systems to avoid this. Full forgiveness may not always be achievable, but most victims come to recognize that to be healthy again they need to deal somehow with these corrosive feelings of anger and hate. Traditional systems of justice do not provide this. Alternative processes, though, often can.

The Canadian Resource Centre for Victims of Crime describes a number of goals of aboriginal justice, and much of what follows owes a debt to the centre's analysis. These goals include healing, harmony, repairing harm, building the community, and bringing the offender back into the circle.

There are a number of mechanisms for achieving these. Peacemaking circles, for example, include a number of different processes: healing circles, community circles, sentencing circles. These endeavour to build community by uncovering underlying problems and restoring balance. Significantly, the primary responsibility for dealing with crime resides in the community, extending beyond the lawbreaker and the victim.

Healing circles try to bring the sense of conflict to a close, allowing participants to express their feelings and get past their hurt and sense of betrayal, while sentencing circles include the traditional trappings of Canadian justice as well as representatives of the community and family, plus the victim and wrongdoer. These all make recommendations to a judge as to disposition or sentence. These may consist of suggestions about probation conditions, or a recommendation for house arrest or prison, or a plea for reparations, or anything else that the participants may deem important to the proceedings. The family and community may also participate in developing a full plan for the offender. Alternatives to prison are often uppermost in these efforts.

I had the privilege of working with an early aboriginal court in Manitoba in the 1990s. This provincial court, presided over by Judge Murray Sinclair, was held in a school on the reserve. The courtroom was smudged before proceedings began. Four elders — two men and two women — attended the proceedings. Their role was to offer advice to the judge on sentencing. Their input was thoughtful and helpful. Incorporating it meant that proceedings took a bit longer, but the outcomes were worth it. Everyone in the room felt that justice was being dispensed in an appropriately deliberate way that was also sensitive to aboriginal values.

I was talking to a young Métis lawyer around this time. We were discussing the considerable shortcomings of European criminal justice and how it served neither aboriginal people nor non-aboriginal people well. In addition to the many problems with the traditional justice system that have been canvassed in this book, the lawyer raised one more. He said the European system fails largely because there have, traditionally, been no women involved in its operations. Until relatively recently, women could not be lawyers or judges or participate in any way in dispensing justice. The system is thus built in a patriarchal, hierarchical way, with no reference to the perspective of women. This lawyer felt that if women had been included, our system would have been much fairer and more humane.

In New Zealand, community conferencing is based on the Maori culture, where they call it family group conferencing (FGC).

The Maori directly involve the accused's family in the effort to hold the offender accountable. He or she is expected to accept personal responsibility and to address the harm done. Australia and other countries have adopted similar processes. Everywhere that we find aboriginal people overrepresented in prisons, such programs are taking hold and establishing viable alternatives.

Community-assisted hearings or releasing circles and healing lodges are also aboriginal programs, but they apply to people who are already serving sentences. Thus, while they offer assistance with rehabilitation and reintegration into the community, they are conducted within prison walls and are not alternatives to prison sentences.

In fact, looking at all of the alternative and interventionist programs and systems described above, it is clear that prison is still the default position. In every case, if the person who caused the harm fails to participate or to complete a program or show progress, he or she is destined for a traditional court where a prison sentence is an option. Moving away from this is difficult, but people who are used to the traditional European way of doing things and encounter RJ for the first time are astounded not only by the new way of thinking, but at the results it can produce.

Judge John Reilly of Alberta wrote a book about this, *Bad Medicine: A Judge's Struggle for Justice in a First Nations Community*. He had come to recognize that our Eurocentric criminal justice system sees wrongdoing as something to be punished, whereas aboriginal people see it more as an illness in need of healing, ignorance in need of teaching. In Canada, where aboriginal youth are more likely to go to prison than to finish Grade 12, he sees the value in trying something other than the Eurocentric approach.

Judge Reilly made reference to one case that showed how a different approach can produce a more fair and healthy result. The victim of a vicious beating had been asking for a prison sentence of one to two years for the person who harmed him. But after participating in a sentencing circle and talking to the wrongdoer and to his community, the victim ended up asking for this person to be set free. The victim was able to forgive the offender, even though he himself would suffer from the physical injuries for the rest of his life. He had let go of his bitterness. The judge thought that his life would be improved as a result.

Another case will be familiar to Canadians. In 1997, teenager Reena Virk was murdered by two others, who were duly convicted and sentenced to prison. Her parents went through the usual stages of grief, including a lot of anger. Then, with the help of RJ facilitators, they sat down and met face to face with one of the murderers, Warren Glowatski. At the end of the meeting, they shook hands and Reena's father told him to go out and do good. The young man had apologized and expressed remorse. The Virks forgave him.

More recently, a young gunman shot and killed four people in La Loche, Saskatchewan. Two of the victims were teachers, and two were brothers. The alleged offender called the mother of the two brothers two days later to apologize to her. He told her that killing the boys was not part of his plan.

The victims' mother responded in a remarkable way. She said, "I may be angry, but I'm not angry at him. I talked to him. He was crying. I forgave him. You can forgive, but you'll never forget." She said that if it were up to her, she would not press charges. "It is true, my whole world is gone, but I know my babies are in a place where there is no pain. I have forgiven you."

We see the same generosity expressed on a regular basis by people who have suffered greatly at the hands of such wrongdoers.

In one of the most notorious cases in Canadian annals, Omar Khadr was held for thirteen years in the prison at Guantanamo Bay, where he was tortured on a regular basis. Asked by his lawyer how he felt about this now, he said that he had no anger. He wanted to become a nurse. He wanted to make sure that nobody else was ever hurt the way he was.

On a much larger scale and on the other side of the world, Rwanda re-established a precolonial justice system to deal with the hundreds of thousands of people involved in the 1994 genocide. Employing the European model would have meant incarcerating virtually all of them, a logistical impossibility and an untenable result. They turned instead to a traditional African system not dissimilar to restorative justice. Baz Dreisinger describes how the 1.2 million people who had killed and maimed victims were tried in "gacacas" ("justice among the grass"). These were truth-telling events, held out in the open on grand lawns. Community-elected judges presided. They sought repentance and reconciliation, and they exacted community-centred labour as the sentence. Today, those who were victims of the genocide but survived and those who did the killing and maiming are largely able to co-exist peaceably in their communities.

For years, one Rwandan victim was terrified that the Hutu would come back from prison to kill her. But she decided that she "couldn't live like that forever." Today, over twenty years later, she is friends with the man who killed nearly all her family and left her for dead. He had written to her from prison and begged her forgiveness. A Christian organization worked with them and created a "reconciliation village" where victims and those who harmed them live together. This highly successful experiment has been referred to as "transitional justice." Reconciliation villages were necessary because many of both the Hutus (the offenders) and the Tutsis (the victims) had nowhere to go after the genocide. On the whole, 92.5 percent of Rwandans feel that reconciliation has been achieved. Surely this is an astonishing result and systems like this beg to be duplicated elsewhere.

ABORIGINAL PEOPLE: THE *GLADUE* CASE

There are many alternatives available to Canadians if we choose to use them. It has already been noted that aboriginal people are vastly overrepresented in Canadian prisons. In 1999 in a case called *R. v. Gladue* the Supreme Court of Canada recognized this anomaly and endorsed a special approach for the sentencing of aboriginal people. This is set out in s. 718.2(e) of the *Criminal Code of Canada*. It requires sentencing judges to consider all sanctions other than prison, and to pay particular attention to the circumstances of aboriginal people in imposing sentence.

The Supreme Court said this section was specifically designed to ameliorate the overrepresentation of aboriginal people in prison and to encourage the use of restorative justice principles in pursuing this end. The court said new provisions of the *Criminal Code* emphasize decreasing the use of incarceration, and that there is an obligation on judges to try to find alternatives to prison, especially where aboriginal people are concerned.

In order to qualify for this process, an offender must self-identify as aboriginal and also agree to accept an RJ remedy and comply with its conditions. The court must consider any adverse impacts upon the particular aboriginal accused person caused by discrimination, abuse, dislocation, substance abuse, and so on. It must then consider appropriate sanctions in view of the person's aboriginal heritage or connection.

Aboriginal accused persons, for their part, must take responsibility for the offence and its consequences on all those affected. They must be prepared to address any underlying factors that might have affected their behaviour so as to prevent any reoffending. Victims are to have an opportunity to say what they think about the use of RJ or not, and to make input into the process. The court may use this process, even for serious offences, where all participants agree.

These principles have been in place for nearly twenty years, but they have not had the desired effect. In fact, the number of aboriginal people in prison has escalated over the past ten years. Between 2005–2006 and 2014–2015, the number of aboriginal men in prison grew by 43.3 percent, while the number of women increased by 70.2 percent. These are alarming figures, and call for courts to start taking seriously and applying principles outlined by the Supreme Court in the *Gladue* case.

HOLLOW WATER FIRST NATION

Attempts to find alternatives to the Eurocentric justice system for aboriginal people who have fallen afoul of the law did not begin with the *Gladue* case. In fact, in the 1980s, long before *Gladue*, the Hollow Water First Nation in Manitoba had begun exploring some other ways of helping both victims of crime and perpetrators in order to achieve healing and peace. At the time, nearly 100 percent of the reserve's population abused alcohol. Unemployment was at 70 percent. And three generations of residents had suffered from sexual abuse or had perpetrated sexual abuse or both. About 70 percent of the community were victims while up to 50 percent had caused this kind of harm. All of the wrongdoers had been victims themselves, and many of them were women. The community rated its community health at zero out of ten.

In the face of these shocking numbers, it was clear that prosecuting all of the accused people under the traditional criminal justice system would entail incarcerating most members of the reserve. Instead, in a move that was revolutionary for the time, the reserve and the criminal justice authorities agreed upon an alternative approach, one that meant doing the hard work needed to retrieve the community's traditional teachings and ceremonies.

With tremendous dedication and fortitude, a small group of leaders, mainly women, reclaimed their traditional way of dealing with misbehaviour. They sat in a circle, established connections with one another, restored the damaged harmony among all parties, and worked to heal and return to balance. This need to restore the community to a well-functioning unit was central to the Hollow Water experiment because the reserve was so small. Everyone knew everyone and most were related. Wrongdoers would be seeing their victims every day once the process was complete.

This process was conducted in conjunction with authorities from the Manitoba court system. It was agreed that when the RCMP had enough evidence to lay a charge against an individual, they would approach the new Community Holistic Circle Healing Program (CHCH). The person who had been charged would then be offered a choice — opt for the traditional Eurocentric court system with its probable prison sentence on conviction, or plead guilty, be placed on probation, and then begin working with the healing circle.

If wrongdoers chose the latter, then they would be required over a period of four months to traverse the "four circles." During this process, they would participate with the CHCH workers, their own family, the victim, and the community. Traditional ceremonies were part of the process, including sweats, the pipe ceremony, smudging, and the passing of the eagle feather. Perpetrators would attend four days of sweat lodge before sentencing, which was done by a provincial court judge (such as Murray Sinclair). There would be a treatment plan and a healing contract. By 2001, CHCH was able to report that only two of the 107 wrongdoers had reoffended. This was six times less than the national average of recidivism for those convicted of sexual abuse.

By 1997, a report on the Hollow Water process posted on the Public Safety of Canada website said that the experiment had been a success, not only in lowering the recidivism rate but also in restoring a devastated community to some semblance of its traditional, functioning, whole self. Local women who participated as CHCH workers in this process reported that the community had regained balance in the four areas essential to their Anishnaabe history: physical, spiritual, mental, and emotional. The importance of elders had been reasserted. Women had regained their traditional strength and position of authority. Men were now showing respect to the women.

The report also praised the Crown attorneys and defence lawyers who had shown such dedication to this task, and such willingness to learn a new process. Participants admitted that they had to be constantly vigilant against intimidation by individual lawbreakers. And there were some for whom prison was still the appropriate response. But for anyone who felt that this process was "the easy way out," wrongdoers were adamant that it was far harder to face their family, their victim, and their community and confess to their crimes than it would have been to spend time in prison.

An extended, extra program such as this costs money, of course. And the workers who had helped to create and run it predicted that a change of government (to one preferring a "tough on crime" agenda) or a reduction in necessary funding would produce problems in delivering the program effectively. Like most small, rural, remote communities — both aboriginal and non-aboriginal — Hollow Water depended on government assistance to deliver essential programs, whether they were for CHCH or water treatment or health care. There was simply no tax base or other source of revenue to pay for these. And it is clear that processing all of these cases through traditional courts would have cost much more money and would have left the community devastated and broken.

The workers were right. Beginning about 1999, the number of sex abuse disclosures dried up, the sentencing circles stopped, and the experiment began to unravel. Observers like Jarem Sawatsky in 2009 blamed a decrease in funding. Workers' salaries had remained the same as they were in early 1990 except for those with university degrees. This was despite cost-benefit analyses that showed that for every $2 spent, $6 to $15 were saved in direct costs.

The deterioration in services was also partly prompted by changes within the reserve. There were new officials at Hollow Water who were less sympathetic to the situation, and a new leader at CHCH had initiated a more hierarchical approach — the antithesis of what an aboriginal community with its circle approach would find workable. Poor relationships with the band council and with the provincial authority, Child and Family Services, further complicated the situation. A growing distrust of the new CHCH workers meant that people were no longer willing to participate in the process.

Still, the Hollow Water community continued to recover its traditions and produced new programs designed to maintain the balance achieved in earlier years. They developed wilderness therapy for youth, a program for women and children, and on-going training for staff.

The efforts of this community to regain its dignity and connectedness has resonated far and wide. Many other communities both in Canada and abroad have sought to implement the new ideas. What is most remarkable about Hollow Water is that it began out of the worst of circumstances as a desperate effort to produce something positive. A few women decided in the 1980s that it was time to get sober and begin to rebuild their dysfunctional community. Once the alcoholism was addressed, other problems revealed themselves, culminating in the realization that sexual abuse was at the bottom of it all. Colonization, residential schools, and the racism of governments and people had brought them to this place.

When Hollow Water First Nation decided to try a new approach in co-operation with the traditional justice system authorities, it was an idea before its time. This version of truth and reconciliation preceded the program in South Africa, the efforts in Rwanda, and the 2008 Canadian commission on residential schools headed up by Justice Murray Sinclair. Those involved in the process still recognized the need to have traditional European-style courts to backstop the toughest cases, but, on the whole, it was a vision of justice that harked back to aboriginal ways, and it produced success.

How to explain, then, why something like Hollow Water's approach has not been taken up and emulated in venues all across the country, building connectedness, restoring families and communities, and diverting those who cause harm from endless circulation in and out of prison? It seems that our criminal justice system has been doing the same thing for so many centuries that it is impossible for people to envision a new way of proceeding. Prison is what we know. We cling to punishment and retribution as if they were positive and enlightened outcomes, when in fact they are regressive, medieval, and harmful to everyone involved. Continuing to support the current system in the face of overwhelming evidence about the harm it causes, and in view of alternative approaches that have shown better results, is a new definition of insanity.

OTHER ALTERNATIVES

There are other alternatives being practised across the country. Vancouver's Downtown Community Court was the first community court in Canada. It opened in 2008, spearheaded by former attorney general Wally Oppal. It is designed to provide an integrated approach for dealing with chronic lawbreakers — about 50 percent of whom have a mental illness or drug dependency or both — who commit minor offences, mostly property crimes, like shoplifting. Local businesses, groups, and residents are engaged, along with fourteen social agencies, in an effort to deal with issues of homelessness, crime, drug dependencies, and mental illness.

In this community court, the accused are encouraged to talk about their lives, something that rarely happens in a traditional court. Most describe lives of pain and suffering, and often describe themselves as "discards" and "castoffs." The community court aims to be less adversarial and more a place where their problems can be dealt with. These are not people who are murdering others or robbing banks, but they may have committed dozens of lesser property crimes, or been found in possession of drugs multiple times. Often their problem can be solved simply with assistance in finding housing, appropriate psychiatric intervention, or treatment for drug and alcohol dependency.

An evaluation of the court showed that it was not particularly successful at providing quicker resolutions than a traditional court, but it was successful at reducing recidivism — no small achievement in a city with the second-highest level of property crime among Canadian cities. And only 4 percent of the community court's cases ever go on to trial in provincial court.

There have been growing pains with the community court, as with any new enterprise. Some people are concerned about high levels of breaches and others say the court is too lenient. But most seem to feel that this is an experiment that deserves to continue, and that it is important to expand the program so clients can be followed after they deal with their charges. A great deal of interest has been expressed in the community court, both here and abroad.

Some observers say that, on the other hand, alternatives to the traditional court system can be counterproductive. They have seen how some of these programs can widen the net, with charges laid in cases where otherwise people would simply be sent on their way by police. For example, if there is a drug-treatment program available, police might be more inclined to lay charges for simple possession of marijuana when otherwise they would send the offender home with a warning.

Drug-treatment courts are also criticized because they have a coercive quality — either an offender agrees to go to the treatment court or he risks a prison sentence in regular court. If he succeeds at treatment, he avoids prison. If he fails to complete the program, he can be sent back to court for sentencing (and prison). Those who work in the drug court in Toronto, though, say that it works, coercive or not.

Toronto's drug-treatment court works with the John Howard Society to ensure good outcomes. JHS finds its clients safe, clean, monitored housing. Fifty-two percent of those who enter the treatment program remain there. As one judge says, you can't make people stop using drugs, but success is more likely in this court than if the offender goes to prison. Behind bars, there is no incentive to quit using and there are lots of drugs available.

People all over the world are interested in this program. And the savings can be enormous. Drug courts cost $12,000 to $20,000 per year per person, compared to the much higher cost of incarceration — from over $100,000 for federal prisoners to more than $50,000 for those in provincial custody.

One of the most noteworthy efforts to shut down prisons by providing alternatives was that provided by Jerome (Jerry) G. Miller in the United States in 1969, long before anyone had tried restorative justice. He took over the Massachusetts youth corrections system, and reduced the number of children in custody from one thousand to forty in four years. Miller placed the rest of the children in community programs, closing virtually all of the large reform schools.

Follow-up research by Harvard University showed that there was no new crime wave as a result, meaning that nearly a thousand young people had been incarcerated for no useful reason. Not only were they imprisoned, these children had been stripped naked and held for days in dark concrete cells, made to drink from toilets, or made to kneel for hours on a stone floor with pencils under their knees. They were also often placed in segregation. They had been brutalized, subjected to torture, deprived of their basic human rights. Miller's program stopped the incarceration of these children and the torture that often accompanied it.

After Miller's intervention not only was there less repeat offending, there was also a decline in the percentage of adult prisoners coming up through the juvenile system. Twenty years later, in Massachusetts there were only twelve youths tried in adult court. This could be compared with Florida, where more than four thousand were tried in adult court that year.

At the time, Florida's population was only about double that of Massachusetts. In the same year, 1989, Massachusetts had dropped to forty-sixth out of the fifty states in number of reported juvenile crimes.

Miller went on to work at Camp Hill in Pennsylvania. The only options for juveniles in this jurisdiction at the time were prison or probation. The panel responsible for deciding which of the two penalties should be imposed had been consistently finding that 95 percent of the children needed to be placed in secure custody. Miller then provided the panel with a third option. He proposed the creation of an individualized plan for each child. Within no time, the panel was finding that only 10 percent needed to be incarcerated.

With startling and positive results like these, it is a wonder that, like Hollow Water, the Miller model has not been enthusiastically adopted and implemented everywhere.

Virtually all of the alternatives described here are backstopped by our traditional court system. That is, if the alternative fails, the wrongdoer stands to be tried and sentenced, possibly to prison, in a criminal court. Is it possible to go a step further and propose a system where prison is no longer the default position for wrongdoing, except for those who are truly dangerous?

As mentioned earlier, many advocates argue that nothing less than "penal abolition" will do. As opposed to "prison abolition," this point of view argues that until we abolish people's inclination to punish, we cannot move forward — merely abolishing prisons will not create the world we all want to live in. They say corporate capitalism is the driving force behind the prison-industrial complex, and until we dismantle that, we cannot claim success.

Many Marxists and faith activists argue that prisons are simply a way of reinforcing the status quo of inequality and brutality. Prisons are about controlling unruly groups, "unacceptable" people, minorities, and the poor. They are not about public safety at all.

It can be agreed that the underlying social conditions that often lead to crime and give prisons their *raison d'être* have to be changed. Those who support "transformational" justice insist that this should be the first and overarching goal, and that without achieving full social justice, we will never be able to dismantle the current system. Prisons assert a need to control; and they do so while failing to treat people with respect, humanity, and dignity. Adherents to transformational justice say where there is no state of justice in the first place, there is nothing to "restore." Yet many of those who promote this view are willing to start with restorative techniques and then move to the ultimate transformation.

Maya Schenwar, in her book *Locked Down, Locked Out: Why Prison Doesn't Work and How We Can Do Better*, describes some efforts at reform as "tinkering towards imperfection." But perhaps being accused of propping up an indefensible regime is the price we have to pay while working for the betterment of those with the most at stake — prisoners, guards, victims, and others. In working to change the system, we cannot afford to sacrifice the good for the sake of the perfect. And we have to act now rather than wait for conditions to be perfect for a wholesale overhaul. The alleviation of current misery and suffering should be paramount.

With eminent optimism, abolitionist Ruth Wilson Gilmore says that "things that take forever can happen overnight." In other words, if we want to do something badly enough, we can summon up the money and the means to do it. She refers to the 2008 bank bailout as an example — somehow, the money was found, almost overnight. However, this was about banks and not about criminals. The likelihood of such a resolution of the problem of prisons is remote, at best.

It is essential that any reforms must neither convey approval of the system nor broaden its reach by net-widening. Building smaller federal prisons for women closer to their homes seemed like a good idea, but there has since been a sharp increase in the number of women imprisoned. Sentencing circles should not be co-opted by police and courts simply as a means of relieving congestion in traditional courts. An ability to ticket behaviour like jaywalking or marijuana possession should not perversely result in police overusing this alternative, ultimately sending people to jail because they are unable to pay fines. The fact that the prison system receives funding for the mentally ill (as it did in the 2017 budget) should not result in more mentally ill people being imprisoned for longer stays in order to receive treatment.

A Canadian website, prisonjustice.ca (in support of prisoners and prison justice activism in Canada), describes imprisonment as morally reprehensible. It recommends the least amount of coercion and intervention with respect to individuals, but the maximum amount of care and services to everyone in society. This is a sensible approach that would deliver alternative modes of justice for most of those who have offended, but also allows for the confinement in humane conditions of those who are dangerous. Where this is necessary, the website suggests the use of halfway houses, community centres, group homes, supervision, intermittent sentences, and so on — not the cages of a maximum-security institution.

The Case for Penal Abolition, edited by W. Gordon West and Ruth Morris, includes a number of essays dedicated to promoting the idea of prison abolition. The consensus of the authors appears to be that abolition will begin when we start to imprison only those who have injured others — not drug users, not technical violators of administrative law, not petty thieves, or people who sleep in the park because they have nowhere else to go.

It makes sense, then, that abolition will have been achieved when only the very dangerous are separated from the public and heavily supervised. Public policy-making based upon these exceptional, sensational, extreme cases must be discouraged. It is essential that we make public policy for the normal case — the ordinary break-in or assault — which can be handled by alternative treatments that do not include prosecutors, courts, judges, and prisons. Then we must find ways of dealing with the exceptional case. We will need to be clear-eyed in identifying those people who pose a real risk to the public and confine them in a way that is secure enough to guarantee public safety and humane enough to guarantee a measure of dignity.

CONCLUSION

If the foregoing tells us anything, it is that merely trying to reform the current prison system will not be enough to undo the harms of incarceration. The punishment approach is easy and popular, but it is fundamentally flawed and immoral. To paraphrase one of our greatest jurists, Louise Arbour, the ultimate product of our criminal justice system — imprisonment — itself epitomizes injustice.

Warehousing people who have transgressed our laws is the "wrong idea from the get-go," says Patricia Monture, a fierce advocate of completely transforming the criminal justice system. As a Haudenosaunee (People of the Longhouse) activist, she has watched her people being incarcerated in ever greater numbers and deplores the system that can seem to find no better way.

It should be clear by now that prisons actually achieve the opposite of what they claim. Prisoners do not learn responsibility in a place where all responsibility is removed from them. They do not learn non-violent ways in a place where violence is ever-present. They do not learn to live peaceably in a community when they have been wrenched from their families and communities and live in fear every waking moment. They do not learn connection with others when they are caught in a maelstrom of splintered relationships and uncertain futures. A life where they can be arbitrarily consigned to the hole, transferred out of the jurisdiction, denied visits, brought up on institutional charges, denied parole — this is not a system that can promote a healthy reintegration to society upon release. Yet we continue to adopt the fiction that prisons can be made to deter criminal behaviour, prevent those incarcerated from committing further offences, and provide victims with some measure of relief.

It bears repeating that the *Criminal Code* requires judges not to send someone to prison "if less restrictive sanctions may be appropriate in the circumstances." It says "all available sanctions, other than imprisonment, that are reasonable in the circumstances and consistent with the harm done to victims or to the community should be considered for all offenders, with particular attention to the circumstances of aboriginal offenders." This is the one principle of sentencing that seems to have been least adhered to. It is as though our adversarial and punitive criminal justice system, with its superprisons and inhumane treatment, is incapable of imagining a response to crime that does not involve locking people up.

It is essential that we stop and rethink the entire colossal superstructure of prisons, immigration detention centres, and other modes of restraint. Something like these may be necessary for the very dangerous, but not for the vast majority of people who currently find themselves caught up in an endless cycle of incarceration.

Kim Pate, with her thirty-five years of experience in prisons, says that people who have worked in the system for any length of time eventually come around to supporting prison abolition. They do so because it is clear that nothing beneficial comes from incarcerating people. But most Canadians have never set foot inside a prison and are never encouraged to think about prisons. Thus, they believe what they are told — that imprisonment is an appropriate response to crime. Even people who regard themselves as progressives often have difficulty accepting the idea of decarceration, much less abolition.

Governments are unlikely to provide leadership on decarceration because being "soft on crime" is a vote-loser. Politicians need to be shown that that there is no such thing as "soft" on crime, but there is "smart" on crime. A different approach will actually produce a measure of success and — even more important to some — will probably save money. Policy-makers need to act upon evidence and not upon the misinformation and prejudices that have so far produced a highly flawed system.

We need to show governments that the staggering amounts of money devoted to incarceration could be reduced and spent on more sensible programs. Our schools and mental health services and other social services would thrive. Families and communities would be strengthened. Restorative justice and other processes would provide care for victims and just sanctions for the people who harmed them. As Canadians, we would be able to hold up our heads in the international community as a wise and caring rather than a heartless, vengeful people. This, after all, is what victims themselves say they want.

The many examples of alternatives to European-style justice should help us move forward in changing our system.

Jerry Miller showed Massachusetts that upwards of a thousand young people had been incarcerated for nothing. Hollow Water First Nation showed that there is a way to deal with serious wrongdoing and serious damage to victims without resorting to prison. Scandinavian countries show us that even for the dangerous, there are ways of confining them that do not involve the dehumanizing conditions common in Canadian prisons. We should be seizing on these examples of unquestioned success and replicating them here. Our public safety depends upon it.

There will never be full agreement on whether or not there is an acceptable level of imprisonment, but there can be fundamental agreement that less is better than more. It is important that we learn how to move outside our comfort zones and work with what may appear to be disparate groups. Gains made by one group should not come at the expense of another. Immigration detention centres are just as important in the decarceration movement as traditional prison settings. We need to work on all of these at once and together.

Grassroots efforts succeed when they build coalitions and strengthen their communities by working together for common goals. Rather than "tearing down prisons," they can work to "crowd prisons out," as Schenwar says. When a community restorative justice process steps in to offer an alternative to prosecution, or when it steps in after conviction to oppose a harsh sentence, it is likely to successfully reduce the number of people in prison. Little by little, the massive prison population will be reduced.

Grassroots organizations can also rally to oppose the building of new prisons, to stop deportations, to change punitive school discipline, to argue for less harsh sentences and less use of solitary confinement, and to resist the addition of offences to the *Criminal Code* that are already covered by existing laws. In all of these ways, we can let governments know that we do not support the incarceration of thousands of Canadians who are no threat to anybody.

In order to tackle decarceration on a larger scale, though, there are a number of things we need to do. To begin with, the large number of mandatory minimum sentences must be eliminated. Canada's minister of justice announced in February 2017 that she was conducting a review of mandatory minimum sentences with a view to eliminating some. The reason she gave for this, though, was not that the sentences often create injustice. It was that they were causing backlogs in the court system: accused persons could no longer make deals with the Crown, so they were opting for trials. This had already resulted in serious offences being stayed. The minister emphasized that for the most serious cases, mandatory minimums were entirely appropriate. Two steps forward, one step back.

It is also necessary to narrow the number of offences on the books and stop criminalizing every wrongdoing that swims into our ken. People should not go to jail for failing to return library books, as was suggested in one U.S. jurisdiction. They should not be criminalized for sleeping on a park bench. Nor should people go to prison for using drugs. The use and abuse of drugs should be in the purview of public health and not of the criminal courts. And administrative offences should of course not attract prison sentences.

On the other hand, there are the truly dangerous. One of my clients, Pierre, had been repeatedly charged with aggravated assault and other violent crimes both inside prison and out. He had been an enforcer for a biker gang during one of the biker wars, and I was sure that he had killed people, although he had never been convicted of murder. He was so dangerous that the correctional officers did not know how to let me safely interview him when we were making a court appearance. Normal rules were that I should be able to protect solicitor-client privilege by talking to him in an enclosed space, ideally an interview room at the court house. But normal rules could not be applied to Pierre. On one occasion, the guards asked me to climb into the back of the paddy wagon and speak to him through the mesh and bullet-proof glass. Then they stood nearby with shotguns and a German shepherd. I doubt if Pierre survived his sentence at Millhaven, but if he did, I hope he was never released.

For these kinds of cases — prisoners who have committed serial sex assault, torture, and murder — some version of separation from society will continue to be necessary. Our task is to develop the means to determine who these people are. Then we must commit to providing them with full human rights and decent treatment while they are in custody.

Another reason for the large numbers of people in custody is that bail provisions are keeping people there while they wait for their charges to be dealt with. They are incarcerated, not because they are a flight risk or a danger to society, but because they can't pay their bail or provide a surety. Clearly, this singles out the indigent, the homeless, and the friendless for differential treatment and results in incarceration for no reason. Large numbers of remand prisoners create overcrowding and resulting horrible conditions for everyone in provincial custody. The situation is manifestly unjust.

One solution for this was available to remand prisoners in Toronto over thirty years ago. A bail project put up bail for accused persons or found someone who would, thus enabling often innocent people to return to their families and jobs until their trials. Such a system needs to be established in every province to reduce these numbers. Also, judges and justices of the peace have to get over their often unreasonable aversion to potential risk. They must stop placing automatic extensive bail conditions on accused persons — conditions that are bound to be breached.

Property theft should rarely if ever attract prison sentences. I say this because in most cases of massive fraud or corporate wrongdoing, wealthy and influential wrongdoers never see the inside of a prison. Instead of arguing that corporate fraudsters should also go to prison for long periods, we should reverse our thinking and deal with minor wrongdoers — shoplifters, cheque kiters, petty fraud artists — without prison sentences. If we are trying to create fairness in the existing criminal justice system, this is the right way to do it.

Another main reason for over-incarceration in Canada is that we fail to release prisoners from their sentences in a timely manner. Under the Conservative government, it became much harder for prisoners to gain release on parole. The parole board has become so risk-averse that many prisoners do not even apply for parole anymore — they know they will not succeed. And most prisoners no longer qualify to apply for parole anyway because the required rehabilitation programs have been drastically reduced. Federal full-parole numbers have dropped by 12 percent in the last five years.

The Conservative government also repealed legislation that allowed for accelerated parole for first-time, non-violent lawbreakers. The immediate result was that many more people, especially women, remained in custody for the full term of their sentences. Such provisions need to be immediately reversed and parole board members must be encouraged to be more reasonable in their assessment of risk. If the CSC is unable to provide sufficient programs to allow prisoners to qualify for parole, then it needs to reassess the need for them and establish a different system for parole qualification. Finally, parole violators should not be returned to prison for technical violations like failing to report a new address or missing an appointment.

The CSC should be releasing more prisoners on compassionate grounds. Many of Canada's federal prisoners are aging, ill, and disabled, and should not be serving out the remainder of their sentences in prison. Similarly, people who are mentally ill should be housed in psychiatric facilities where they can be treated properly and where they are not under threat of violence because of their illness. And there could be mass releases of certain categories of prisoners: those who are convicted of non-violent property offences, victimless drug infractions, administrative transgressions, and many other kinds of offences. This is being done elsewhere without negative consequences, and Canada should be following suit.

In addition to efforts to release prisoners and shorten sentences there must be a coordinated effort at public education. The media have been complicit with governments in making the public fearful of violent crime by exaggerating its scope and seriousness. It bears repeating that crime has been declining for years, including violent crime. Our communities are safe, and most people tell pollsters that they feel safe. However, there is a lot of ignorance about the prison system and how it works.

Without actually going into prison, it is hard for the average person to fully understand how violent and soul-destroying it is. We need to find ways to communicate this.

A new book by Robert Clark, a thirty-year career officer with the CSC, provides an excellent overview of the federal prison system as he experienced it in Kingston. *Down Inside: Thirty Years in Canada's Prison Service*, is a searing indictment of the system, replete with horrific stories of life "down inside" for both staff and prisoners. He lauds the hard work of the many men and women who try to achieve high standards in the system, but he doubts that real positive change is possible.

Clark says the culture of the CSC — what he calls the culture of collective indifference — is too deeply entrenched to change. He believes that conditions are worse today than when he left the service in 2009, and those were worse than when he arrived in 1980. The evidence of Clark's experience is invaluable in understanding what our prison system has become. As one who worked within the system for so long, he has a credibility that will recommend itself to readers.

Politicians will never be convinced to change the system substantially, much less provide an alternative system, until their constituents push them hard. In order for average citizens to promote this cause, they will have to first understand that prisons are unnecessary, counterproductive, expensive, and inhumane. Then they have to be shown alternatives that work and encouraged to envision a whole new system. Finally, they have to see that the way we deal with wrongdoing is a measure of our humanity. As a civilized people, we cannot continue down this road. It leads to a dark place and it tarnishes us all.

ACKNOWLEDGEMENTS

I would like to thank the many people who helped me shape this book in a way that I hope makes a controversial argument both readable and convincing.

The personnel at Dundurn have been stellar, especially Patrick Boyer, who is the general editor of the Point of View series, developmental editor Dominic Farrell, managing editor Kathryn Lane, project editor Elena Radic, and copy editor Laurie Miller. Many thanks to the others who worked on text and presentation.

I want especially to acknowledge the people who took time from very busy schedules to comment on the manuscript. Bill Bogart, author of *Off the Street: Legalizing Drugs*, gave valuable advice on the content and arrangement of the book. Senator Kim Pate contributed comments based upon her many years of experience as former executive director of the Canadian Association of Elizabeth Fry Societies. Paul Ropp helped me understand recent developments in corrections and focus my argument more directly on the issues presented by the system. Dr. Anthony Doob offered sage advice once again, for which I am grateful. Finally, thank you to Catherine Latimer, executive director of the John Howard Society, who graciously agreed to provide a foreword for this book.

I want to thank my family. They taught me that everyone deserves a second chance.

John, you are my rock. Thank you for helping me work through another book, even while writing your own. You have my gratitude and my love.

BIBLIOGRAPHY

Alexander, Michelle. *The New Jim Crow: Mass Incarceration in the Age of Colorblindness*. New York: The New Press, Revised Edition, 2012.

Arbour, Louise. *Report of the Commission of Inquiry into Certain Events at the Prison for Women in Kingston*. Ottawa: Public Works and Government Services Canada, 1996.

Boyer, J. Patrick. *A Passion for Justice: How "Vinegar Jim" McRuer Became Canada's Greatest Law Reformer*. Toronto: Dundurn Press, 2008.

Christie, Nils. *Crime Control as Industry: Towards Gulags, Western Style*. London: Routledge, Third Edition, 2000.

Clark, Robert. *Down Inside: Thirty Years in Canada's Prison Service*. Fredericton, NB: Goose Lane Editions, 2017.

Clear, Todd R. *Imprisoning Communities: How Mass Incarceration Makes Disadvantaged Neighborhoods Worse*. Oxford: Oxford University Press, 2007.

Correctional Service of Canada Review Panel. *A Roadmap to*

Strengthening Public Safety. Ottawa: Minister of Public Works and Government Services, 2007.

CR10 Publications Collective. *Abolition Now! Ten Years of Strategy and Struggle Against the Prison Industrial Complex*. Oakland: AK Press, 2008.

Davis, Angela Y. *Are Prisons Obsolete?* New York: Seven Stories Press, 2003.

Dreisinger, Baz. *Incarceration Nations: A Journey to Justice in Prisons Around the World*. New York: The Other Press LLC, 2016.

Forman, James Jr. *Locking Up Our Own: Crime and Punishment in Black America*. New York: Farrar, Straus and Giroux, 2017.

Gendreau, P., C. Goggin, and F.T. Cullen. *The Effects of Prison Sentences on Recidivism*. Ottawa: Solicitor General of Canada, 1999.

Hinton, Elizabeth. *From the War on Poverty to the War on Crime: The Making of Mass Incarceration in America*. Cambridge, MA: Harvard University Press, 2016.

Jackson, Michael. *Prisoners of Isolation: Solitary Confinement in Canada*. Toronto: University of Toronto Press, 1983.

———. *Justice Behind the Walls: Human Rights in Canadian Prisons*. Toronto: Douglas and McIntyre, 2002.

———. "Reflections on 40 Years of Advocacy to End the Isolation of Canadian Prisoners," *Canadian Journal of Human Rights* 4, no. 1 (2015): 57–87.

Jackson, Michael, and Graham Stewart. *A Flawed Compass: A Human Rights Analysis of the Roadmap to Strengthening Public Safety* (September 25, 2009). CBC.ca/News, 2009. Available at SSRN: https://ssrn.com/abstract=1881036.

Kilgore, James. *Understanding Mass Incarceration*. New York: The New Press, 2015.

MacGuigan, Mark. *Report of the House of Commons Sub-Committee on the Penitentiary System in Canada.* Ottawa: Ministry of Supply and Services, 1977.

Mallea, Paula. *Aboriginal Law: Apartheid in Canada?* Brandon: Bearpaw Publishing, 1994.

———. *Fearmonger.* Toronto: James Lorimer and Company, 2011.

———. *The War on Drugs: A Failed Experiment.* Toronto: Dundurn Press, 2014.

Morris, Norval, and David J. Rothman, editors. *The Oxford History of the Prison.* Oxford: Oxford University Press, 1995.

Office of the Correctional Investigator. *Annual Reports.* Ottawa: Her Majesty the Queen in Right of Canada.

www.prisonjustice.ca.

www.radicalcriminology.org.

Reilly, John. *Bad Medicine: A Judge's Struggle for Justice in a First Nations Community.* Calgary: Rocky Mountain Books, 2010.

Sawatsky, Jarem. *The Ethic of Traditional Communities and the Spirit of Healing Justice: Studies from Hollow Water, the Iona Community, and Plum Village.* London: Jessica Kingsley Publishers, 2009.

Waller, Irvin. *Less Law, More Order: The Truth About Reducing Crime.* Ancaster: Manor House Publishing, 2011.

West, Gordon W., and Ruth Morris, editors. *The Case for Penal Abolition.* Toronto: Canadian Scholars' Press Inc., 2000.